A HISTORY OF THE NORMANTON METHODIST CIRCUIT

Ronnie Aitchison

Dedication

My thanks are due to the people who gave me their time and memories, without whom this would have been impossible. In particular Margaret and Bev Davies, Stephen Furness, Gillian Dennison and Ian Hollingsworth. The staff at the West Yorkshire Archives at Wakefield have offered unfailing assistance throughout this project.
My wife has given unstinting support and invaluable editorial assistance.

First edition published by Furness and Aitchison, Normanton, West Yorkshire

ISBN 978-1-4716-7624-6

This Second Edition April 2012
Published by Lulu.Com

Contents

INTRODUCTION

My intention is to tell the story of the development of the Normanton Methodist Circuit. As with most such stories it is not a simple linear history, it is much more complex than that. It is not the story of one group, it tells of the Primitive Methodist Circuit in Normanton and the Wesleyan churches in the area which grew alongside them. All of these were offshoots of Wakefield Methodism. There were also United Free Methodists within the area and, of course, despite the name Normanton covers congregations in Altofts, Streethouse and the villages of Sharlston and New Sharlston.

By its very nature this story will involve some understanding of the growth of communities and industries throughout the area involved.

The starting point was not easy to define. The Primitive Circuit, in 1942, marked its centenary with a major celebration, but the Circuit had not become a separate entity until 1879. The Wesleyans broke away from Wakefield to form a circuit centred on Rothwell struggling with identity and purpose for decades. Despite the national agreement on Methodist Unity in 1932, it was quite some years before a "Methodist" circuit came into being in Normanton which seems to have been the story throughout the country.

This covers a period when the two denominations moved from independence and a degree of distance between them, up to the gradual move to union and the long period of rapprochement which lead to local amalgamation.

One of the surprising discoveries to me was the attitude to Holy Communion in the Primitive Methodist Circuit. Having always heard that, "Prims paid less regard to Communion" to find the emphasis on the sacrament throughout this whole period was interesting. Monthly communion services were laid down by the Quarterly Meeting from the beginning and Local Preachers were disciplined for the offence of neglecting the means of grace more often than any other cause. This was so, right up to amalgamation.

Direct references to a "Head Church" were also interesting. When amalgamation was being mooted discussion as to which should be the "Head Church" featured powerfully in this matter.

In both Wesleyan and Primitive churches and circuits there was a much greater role played by lay members than would be found today, but of course that went alongside a remarkable acceptance of responsibility. I doubt if today's circuit stewards would feel it was their duty to fund the circuit deficit in difficult times for example.

Local Preachers too seem to have had an even greater commitment to the role than we do today and much more was demanded of them. With no personal transport, long working weeks and low incomes, these early preachers demonstrated a remarkable commitment and the church expected no less.

My Sources

I am grateful to all those who have shared their memories with me and pointed me in the right direction. The encouragement I received helped in the long hours searching the Archives.

Almost all of this book is based on the Minutes of Quarterly, Circuit and Church meetings consulted in the Wakefield branch of the West Yorkshire Archives. Sadly there are missing records, gaps and in some cases very brief entries in the Minutes. I hope I have been able to do them justice.

CHAPTER ONE

Beginnings

In September 2011 a new circuit, the Aire and Calder came into being. This is an amalgamation of four circuits - Wakefield - Pontefract and Normanton - Castleford - Ossett and Horbury. This little history tells the story of the struggles, through separation, growth and eventual amalgamation of one part of that new entity. The story starts in the early 1800s as the strong Methodist denominations centred in Wakefield stretched out towards the growing mining villages on its edges and culminates in the 1947 amalgamation of Primitive and Wesleyan congregations which created the Normanton Methodist Circuit.

Primitive Methodist Beginnings

Normanton in 1842 was a small town with a population of only 250. The old town had been a quiet place with a parish church and a grammar school, but little of consequence in the way of industry until the railway came in 1840. Perhaps it was the signs of growth that had come with that venture which prompted the Wakefield Primitive Methodist Circuit to send the Rev J. Toulson and a small group to mission to the town. Their efforts were rewarded by some success, in particular by the enthusiastic response of Mr and Mrs John Lee. Toulson and his group preached at the old village cross, opposite the Black Swan Inn, roughly where the police station now stands. There is no record of numbers involved in this early effort, but the Lees were so impressed that they offered the use of their house to hold services and class meetings. The work continued and developed with the support of Mrs Lee in particular for many years. It was strong enough by 1868 that the Society was able to build a wooden chapel on a piece of land which they leased in Woodhouse, where the First Board House School was later built (this is now small business units). The Society struggled a little at first in their new home, but seems to have prospered as the town did.

By 1871 Normanton had a population of 3,448, and considerable industry. The railway station was the hub of a great deal of traffic, both passenger and freight, there was a busy iron and steel foundry built between the station and the old town and mining had grown and developed at several centres around Normanton. Undoubtedly this growth had brought people to the town with a connection to the Primitive Methodists as well as a new source of mission, and in 1874 the society built a new brick Church further up Wakefield Road on the site of the present Methodist Church. This new building had cost them £1,442 and was to become the centre of an active Primitive Circuit in the coming years.

The Quarterly Minutes of the Normanton section of the Wakefield Circuit in December 1878 list regular services at Normanton, Altofts, Streethouse, New Sharlston and Sharlston Common. Alongside these were various mission services at Beckbridge and St John's Terrace within the environs of Normanton itself and at Lee Brigg[1] on the road to Altofts. With total numbers under 200 members, this may seem ambitious, but there was clearly a burgeoning cause in the area and, while Normanton only had 72 members on its register it records an attendance of 200 at its main services. Altofts at this time was the larger church with a membership of 130 and 300 attending the services. By the spring of 1879

---

[1] I have used this form in all cases other than a quotation from the minutes. The area has been called Lee Bridge, and earlier Lee's Bridge, but Lee Brigg is the most usual form during the period of this history.

a meeting of the leaders of the section agreed a plan to become a separate section with the Rev Mr Waite as Superintendent. It was stated that there were 193 members in the new circuit but the minutes also separately include a number of persons on trial. As a record of the history of the Normanton Methodist Circuit, this has to be the starting point, but not the only new start.

Wesleyan Methodism

Wakefield Wesleyan Methodist Circuit had a foot in the same door. In the same year the Primitive Circuit sent their mission to Normanton the Wesleyans built their first church in the area. Altofts had appeared on the Wakefield Wesleyan plan as early as 1809. At that time services were held in a building at Greystones opposite where the present church building now stands. These meetings continued until about 1838 with only a short break in the early 1820s. The first Church building was completed in 1842, at a cost of £329 8s 10d (£329 45p in today's terms). The value of the land was given as £20. In this period, the Wakefield Wesleyan circuit had one other Society in the Normanton area, this being at Sharlston. In this mining village, with a strong Christian management, albeit Congregationalist, worship was encouraged. The Wesleyan Circuit had services from 1813. These were held in a cottage belonging to the mine company. The membership at both the Altofts and the Sharlston Churches fluctuated wildly. In 1850 Altofts showed a membership of three and Sharlston 13; by 1855 Altofts had grown to 12 and Sharlston to 50. Ten years later Altofts had again increased its membership to 44 while Sharlston languished at 10. How such a small and erratic membership as that at Altofts could support a Church is amazing.

Normanton appears in the Wesleyan records for the first time in 1867 with a plan to build a school. The Wesleyans had been holding meetings in a room at Normanton station since 1861 when a disastrous accident had initiated what became the Railway Servants Missions. A meeting held in March 1868 confirmed the plan to build in Normanton and a Church was built in Wakefield Road. This new society is shown with 10 members. The faith which is demonstrated in this move is rewarded with a rapid and steady growth, 48 members in 1870 and 100 shown on the records for 1881.

The Sharlston congregation in the meantime was steadily reducing. There were two Methodist meetings in Sharlston, Wesleyan and Primitive meeting in the two cottages. In 1868 the mine owners decided to provide a dedicated building for worship in the village which became a Methodist Church. The worshippers were asked to vote on which denomination the building should belong to, the Primitives winning this vote. It is impossible to say whether a declining membership in the Wesleyan congregation or a growing Primitive congregation swayed this decision, but as will be seen later, a unified congregation was to be a successful one for many years.

In March 1892 a special circuit meeting was held at Rothwell in the Wakefield Wesleyan Circuit. This meeting was attended by all four ministers, Revds H.O. Rattenbury, Superintendent, Alfred Elvidge, I. R. Sharpley and William Stewart, along with both circuit stewards and 75 members. It was said to be the largest meeting ever held and was called to discuss the division of the circuit. The proposal, instigated by the stated desire of Normanton for an increase in ministry, was brought to the meeting by one of the Stewards, Mr H. Richardson. Despite the outcome of the meeting, this desire was to be a bone of contention again and again.

The proposal was that this new circuit was to be called Leeds Rothwell and to consist of Rothwell, Normanton, Stanley, Oulton, Woodlesford, Carlton, Altofts and Ouzlewell Green. The motion was carried by 69 votes for, three against and three abstaining. A resolution was sent to the Leeds District asking for the services of a young man for the ensuing year and offering a pledge to take on a married man when the year was ended.

With the Leeds District Meeting approving the scheme in May 1892 the way was clear for the new circuit to come into being.

This new circuit was launched with much celebration and a weekend of activity. The inaugural public meeting was chaired by Mr Joseph Marsden of Normanton and addressed by Revd Professor J. S. Banks, Professor of Theology at Headingley College and the singing was led by the choirs, numbering 80 persons, of all the churches.

The celebration service was led by the new Superintendent, Revd William Stewart, who was to live at Rothwell and Revd Herbert Nicholls, who was stationed in Normanton. The new Circuit, which claimed a membership of 494 with 90 juveniles and 35 on trial, took on the cost of a new house in Normanton at £500 to be paid over four years. The provision of this along with a salary of £170[2] for the Superintendent and £150 for the second minister were the principal outgoings for which this membership became responsible.

---

[2] £170 in 1890 would have the buying power of £10,180 in today's money.

CHAPTER TWO

Early growth and struggles

It is probably fair to say that the establishment of the new Primitive Methodist Circuit was a less troubled project than was its sister Wesleyan circuit. The minutes of the Society meetings move smoothly from arrangements for outreach in December 1878 to a decision to become a separate circuit with Revd Waite as Superintendent in March 1879.

That December meeting made arrangements for what were clearly regular services at Normanton, Altofts, Streethouse, New Sharlston, Sharlston Common and St John's Terrace. Despite the seemingly burgeoning growth, there were only three Churches; Normanton, which was seen as the main church of the new circuit, Lock Lane in Altofts and the New Sharlston building. This last was the property of the mining company and remained so for some years to come, but was dedicated to worship provided by the Primitive Methodist preachers, and home of the Sharlston Primitive Methodist Society.

Buildings as such were always an ambition, but the reality lay in societies. It was in the laity that the strength of the Primitive Methodist circuits was found. Normanton had come into being as an independent circuit through the will and commitment of the lay leadership in the area. Its continued growth can be traced to the commitment of stewards and members of classes willing to band together to form a society in a particular community and thereafter strive to fund the building of a Church as their dedicated place of worship.

The societies at Sharlston Common, Beckbridge and St John's remained active for some time without the advantage of buildings and Lee Brigg (Leebridge as the genteel recorder of the Normanton Minutes names it) was an endeavour which came off and on the plan over the years.

Growing pains

The new circuit had a membership of 193 along with about 20 members on trial. This "members on trial" status remained a feature of the Primitive Methodist system until after Methodist Union. The understanding seemed to be one step on from an adherent but not yet a full member. From the records it is clear that not all of these "on trials" came into full membership.

The minister's salary was set at £21 per quarter and he received £1 6s for each of his two children. This children's allowance was a normal part of the remuneration system for ministers and struggling circuits might request a "young man", not necessarily a probationer, who would be paid substantially less and would be required to lodge with a member of the church. The minister and his family were provided with a house although, at this time, the new circuit did not own a property and rented a house, No 3 The Grove, Normanton, at the cost of £4 4s 6d per quarter.

At the first Quarterly Meeting two Society stewards were appointed for Normanton but one declined to work with the other and this situation continued for most of the following year. Although the new circuit did not officially come into being until after the June Conference, the society in Normanton appears to have operated as though it were a circuit for at least a year prior to this. The Quarterly Meeting heard reports on the preachers, organised the plan and heard disciplinary proceedings on preachers and members before going into general session. Although these meetings were normally chaired by the minister, a steward would preside if the minister were not available. The plan included Camp Meetings in various open spaces once a quarter while the organising chapel would have a love feast to coincide with the Camp Meeting. This was so even in the areas where there was no formal church in the early days. Some of today's Methodists who claim a Primitive tradition might be surprised to hear that a service of Holy Communion was planned at each place of worship once a month. It was this practice which necessitated services being planned in the afternoon and evening in the smaller places.

The circuit finances were precarious from the start. The income from the six contributing societies was £19 16s 3½d the remainder listed as deficiency. Dealing with the deficiency was a struggle and could be met by special efforts, or often, by remaining in debt. There is no suggestion that the minister did not receive his salary, but evidence that the stewards personally carried the debt for periods of time. Despite this precarious situation, there were huge leaps of faith. In July 1879 Sharlston Common was given permission to buy land for the building of a church, a project which was to take some years to come to fulfilment, but the September Quarterly Meeting pledged to pay off the Sharlston Common debt in six weeks.

Early in 1879, while still a part of the Wakefield circuit, Streethouse had gained permission to buy land for the construction of a church and had bought a piece of land from a Mr Graves at 2s 6d a foot. This was not to be an easy or comfortable undertaking but was an example of the determination and commitment of communities to have a worshipping congregation within their own boundaries.

In March 1879 Lee Bridge was removed from the plan. A renewed mission had been set up in this community half way between Normanton and Altofts with services on Sunday afternoon and Thursday evening but, despite these efforts, no great headway was made. It seems certain that there were members of the Normanton Society resident in this area who had acted as the core of a hoped for new congregation, but this was not to be.

The Quarterly Meetings in 1880 bring change and a rash of troubles. In March the circuit decided to invite the Revd Henry Crabtree to be Superintendent from the following connexional year. While it was quite normal for ministers to move on after one or two years, it is possible that the fact that Mr Crabtree was a childless widower while Mr Waite now having three children each receiving the child allowance, may have been a consideration with the precarious state of the circuit finances. Further evidence for such a need is found in that Revd Crabtree offered to accept £23 a quarter (stated as salary) which was a decrease of £2. To offer some perspective, a miner in a skilled position could earn £19 a quarter and lesser skilled workers as little as £13. At the beginning of the year the circuit recorded 201 members but only reported 180 to Conference, this seems to have been a regular practice. At the year's end they were still recording 201 but had six members on trial.

Throughout 1880 the preachers' meeting dealt with disciplinary matters. Each occasion in the minutes lists the name as well as the offence. The first of these concerns a preacher found guilty of making an indecent proposal to a member of the congregation at Streethouse; he was suspended from communion duties for twelve months. Another was removed from the plan owing to rumours of domestic difficulties. As it is noted that he has left the family home these would seem to be serious. In December a committee was set up to investigate a preacher who was accused of improper behaviour. He was found to have visited public houses and to have become intoxicated on some occasions. Since he does have business in the public houses it is decided to send a letter reducing his appointments on the following plan. Clearly there was a different mindset in the 1880s if reducing a preacher's appointments was seen as a punishment!

The Beckbridge class was now officially separate from the Normanton Society, this being the first step towards forming a new society. The preaching services were held in the home of a Mrs Williamson. Clearly, despite the fact that the circuit was still short of funds, there was a spirit of hope and adventure. Perhaps this was embodied in the start up of the Band of Hope which now, at the end of 1880, had commenced occasional meetings at Normanton and Streethouse.

The following year was quieter, but not without event. A dispute had arisen at Sharlston Common with regard to the proposed building. Work had been started and a bill received in regard to this work from a Mr Reid. The difficulty was that this had not been authorised by the circuit and, in view of the shortage of funds, the venture had created a problem. This difficulty was to simmer away for some time to come.

Mrs Williamson was written to, requesting that she allow the preaching services to continue in her house at Beckbridge.

An odd little note occurs, which is repeated throughout the following years, the Quarterly Meeting records that several societies are "given permission" to go out singing at Christmas to raise funds. It would seem that all fund raising measures other than direct giving of the members required circuit meeting authorisation and such events were dealt with within strict criteria. There seems to have been some stigma attached to fundraising beyond the congregation.

Fluctuating fortunes

In the next few years the Circuit Minutes record swings of fortune, changes of personnel and circumstances throughout the circuit. Most remarkable was that the membership had increased in 1882 by 93, bringing the total up to 300.

When speaking of Altofts the minutes normally refer to Lock Lane (Altofts), a thriving small church at the foot of the village but very much part of the Normanton Circuit. There were regular attempts to mission in Lee Brigg and in upper Altofts village, shown on the plan as Altofts Common. In March 1882 the services which had been held in Mr Jones's house were stopped. This was not to be an end to the Altofts venture as a proposal was accepted for a new church at Altofts.

1882 was to be a year of new starts for churches. The superintendent was given permission to form a trust for a new place of worship at Sharlston Common. This was not about authorising the situation with Mr Reid, which was a dispute which was to linger. What was proposed was a new start with an elected board of Trustees. It was to take three years and several false starts before this was to come into being. A similar proposition was agreed for Beckbridge and a fund was commenced for "a cheap place of worship" there.

New Sharlston, meanwhile, had continued to worship in the building belonging to Sharlston colliery, but the manager was now anxious that there should be a formal agreement signed with regard to the occupancy of the church.

By the end of the year Altofts Common had the use of a preaching room in the village for which it had borrowed a set of forms from Lock Lane and it is back on the plan.

Despite these apparent signs of improvement there were still financial struggles. The December accounts show that Mr Crabtree was paid 12s 1d back salary, this sort of entry appearing in each of the next few quarters, this despite his having accepted a decreased salary at the very beginning of his appointment.

Individual churches also showed signs of money problems. The Streethouse Trustees, in March 1883, leased the church to the Streethouse School Board for twelve months for an annual rent of only £10 and the Quarterly Meeting decided that each society in the circuit should hold a special collection for Streethouse. With all the best will in the world such a collection could only raise a very few pounds in a circuit which had difficulty raising the minister's salary.

Although there was now a formal Board of Trustees for Sharlston Common, the Circuit held a special meeting concerning Mr Reid's claim concerning the plans he had prepared for a church in the village. This continued to be inconclusive and the matter was later the cause of a District investigation.

St John's Terrace continued on the plan and the services were still held in the front room of a member, at No 53. Although there were a considerable number living in St John's Terrace, they were largely Irish colliers imported to work at St John's Colliery on the Newland Hall estate. The Roman Catholic Church had also built a mission church in the vicinity. Despite these difficulties the Primitive Methodist circuit continued with its mission for another fifteen years, and at this June 1883 meeting, it started to raise funds for a wooden mission hall in the Terrace.

Two or three of the decisions taken at this meeting offer interesting insights from a present day perspective. The first is an odd use of language, at least to our understanding, the Trustees at Normanton Church are given permission to *beg* for the building of a new school room and then the Streethouse Trustees were given permission to *beg* for the church. Strictly speaking, this is a perfectly correct use of the word, because they were going to solicit donations for their purpose from those beyond the church congregation. Churches today mask most such fund raising in the guise of entertainments or coffee mornings etc. In the nineteenth century they seem to have been very honest in their usage and in their understanding of what they were doing. At the same time the meeting appointed two stewards to inspect the superintendent's house and to sign his credentials "if the house is clean to their satisfaction". The Superintendent was preparing to move to another appointment and would be required to present acceptable credentials to his new circuit if he were to be accepted. The following meeting notes that the incoming Superintendent's credentials were accepted. These papers went with preachers, both itinerant and local, throughout their life and recorded their qualifications, acceptance into office and conduct throughout their service.

The collection taken at the leaving service for Mr Crabtree was to be used towards the furnishing of the preacher's house. In the event this went to the purchase of a bed and some other furnishings.

This, the last meeting presided over by Mr Crabtree, also decided that no pieces were to be read or recited at entertainments in churches without the approval of the leaders' meeting. Whatever had brought the meeting to make such a ruling seems to have occurred at a Streethouse event, but the minutes are not specific in this respect.

The new superintendent came to Normanton in September of 1883 although his credentials were not to be accepted until the December meeting. The Revd Philip Thornton Yarker, a comparatively young man of 36, came from Barrowford in Lancashire. He was married and brought with him two children both of whom had been born in Normanton. Sadly, he and his wife had recently lost their youngest child. With this new start, the circuit agreed to pay the usual salary of £25 per quarter and the children's allowance of £1 6s per child.

His first meeting was filled with the usual matters of local preachers and plan arrangements, but included permission given to Beckbridge to erect a wooden church, purchased from Normanton Trust, on the land they had acquired in Castleford Road.

Sharlston Common were also given permission to build, the first proper step to a new church. In the meantime they had established a reasonably active Band of Hope. There were other Bands at Normanton Church and occasional meetings at Streethouse. The Quarterly Meeting gave permission for the purchase of a fife and drums for the formation of a band within the Band of Hope at Sharlston. The fife is to be the property of Sharlston and the three drums to remain circuit property.

Mr Yarker had brought a new rule to the meeting. Baptisms, which had not been formal plan occasions in the past, were to be at Normanton on Sunday mornings and at the other places of worship on Sunday afternoons, as arranged. In this decision, baptism is referred to as an ordinance rather than a sacrament. It seems that "sacrament" at this time was used solely for Holy Communion.

Camp meetings had been a part of the activity of the circuit from its formation, but now five camp meetings were planned for the coming summer with invited preachers for most, in particular an application had been made for the Railway Lay Preachers to visit the circuit during one of the meetings. The railway was a major employer in Normanton with considerable traffic, over a million tons of traffic used the sidings each year and there were 100 engines permanently located at Normanton. The Railway Lay Preachers were part of the mission to railway workers and active in Yorkshire.

As an aside, I must confess how easy it is to confuse terms at this distance. One of the first mentions of Methodism in Normanton is around meetings held in a room at Normanton Station, a presence which continued for some years. My confusion arose through the use of "Station meeting" and "Station school" in the minutes over the next decade. It was quite some time before I realised that "Station" was the term used by the Primitive Methodists at that time where we would use circuit.

One of the features of the Circuit Minutes in the nineteenth century is the way in which matters reach a decision in one meeting and then there is a change in opinion at the next. In March 1884 it was decided that no preachers should be planned at Altofts Common, but in the

September meeting this preaching place was back on the plan. Between the two decisions, Mr Yarker had been in correspondence with a Mr Jones of Altofts with regard to the use of the mission room at Silkstone Row and it had been agreed to hold services if they could get use of the room. The negotiations at Beckbridge had also faltered. The Quarterly Meeting, in September, considered the price of the land needed, at 3s 6d per yard, to be excessive but permission had still been sought from the District to build a wooden place of worship. At the same meeting a report was made on another Beckbridge difficulty; a local preacher from the Beckbridge society was the subject of a disciplinary hearing and at the following Quarterly Meeting he was removed from the plan the fault, failing to attend the means of grace.

New vigour

Mr Yarker was to receive annual invitations to remain in the circuit for the next three years. It is likely that he took the decision, in1887, that it was time to move on. Ministers, at this time, were expected to be itinerant and despite his success and seeming popularity, it must have been quite wearing facing the annual reinvitation at the Quarterly Meetings. During the pastorate of this minister most of the circuit churches saw growth and building work did move forward despite what seem to have been regular setbacks.

The membership in the circuit in March 1885 was:

Normanton	97
Altofts (Lock Lane)	43
St John's	23
Altofts Common	8
New Sharlston	55
Streethouse	23
Sharlston Common	17
Beckbridge	16

By September 1887, at the end of Mr Yarker's time it stood at:

Normanton	145
Altofts (Lock Lane)	38
St John's	18
Altofts Common	10
New Sharlston	82
Streethouse	54
Sharlston Common	32
Beckbridge	15

Normanton, the principal church in the circuit, had shown a significant increase, as had New Sharlston and Streethouse. Each of these areas had seen an expansion of population and had been able to bring a proportion of these newcomers into their congregation. There was constant growth in employment at the railway yards in Normanton and the mines at Sharlston and Streethouse were also expanding.

Lock Lane, Altofts, was in a different situation. On the very edge of the circuit and with Wesleyan churches both to the east and the west of its centre of activity, it was less well situated to take advantage of a growing population. The mine at the lower end of the village might have seemed a good opportunity for evangelisation, but there were some barriers to

Lock Lane

success there. The mine owners were Christian and keen

that their workers should have the opportunity to belong to a Christian community, but most of the miners had been brought in from the Shropshire area where Wesleyan Methodism was more prevalent and the mine owners built them a church which fell naturally into the sphere of the Castleford Wesleyan Circuit. The faithful folk of Lock Lane maintained their worship and presence, but all attempts by the circuit to expand in the village floundered. Altofts Common, which had come back on to the plan in 1884, closed again in 1887. The services were to be discontinued and Mr Jones, whose premises they had used, was informed of the cessation. The decision then became odd in the extreme. The name of the preaching place was not to come off the plan, but the cupboard and benches were presented to Beckbridge and the hymn books were divided between Beckbridge and Streethouse. The harmonium was sold. The ten remaining members were informed by the new minister, the Revd William Bennett, that they should join another society or constitute themselves as a separate society.

During these two years, Beckbridge and Sharlston Common, with several ups and downs in their fortunes, succeeded in building their first church premises. At Beckbridge there was some optimism shown in 1885 as they planned a reopening service and got the wooden building underway, but funds were still a problem, and a year later they were asking permission to spend a further £20 on the church. The funds had been borrowed from the District Chapel committee and in January 1887 they were having to request an extension of one month to raise half the total cost. In February they had raised all but £5. Doubtless this new venture is what triggered the discussions with Castleford circuit regarding circuit boundaries. To modern eyes this area is clearly a part of Normanton Town. But Castleford stretched into Whitwood and seems to have claimed all of the neighbouring housing. An agreement was reached to define the boundary[3] which was set at the end of Prospect Terrace in Castleford Road.

Sharlston Common was in a similar situation. Unlike Beckbridge it had not been able to acquire land in ownership, but had been given permission by the circuit to lease a piece of land on which to build their wooden chapel. The land rent was to be £1. 10s per year[4] with an initial charge of one and a half guineas for the cost of making the lease. As with Beckbridge they found themselves seeking an extension, this time of three months, although they were able to bring the debt down to £4[5] within a month.

Much more ambitious were the plans at Normanton for the building of a new school. The district had already sanctioned the spending of £700 pounds on this project and the bulk of the work had been done by the middle of 1884, but further work on remodelling the interior took place in 1885 and beyond. A sign of the confidence at this, the principal church in the town, was the decision to buy hymn books for visitors.

Circuit growth, both in numbers and churches, prompted the appointment in 1886 of a committee responsible for the investigations regarding the purchase of a minister's house. The initial proposal was to buy a parcel of land on which to build. A variety of pieces of land were considered, but no decision was taken on this route.

The minutes of the Local Preachers' meeting held before the Quarterly Meeting in Decemb er 1886 record the answers to two of the questions addressed to a preacher on trial. The first answer he gave was, "That by the witness of the Spirit the justified person is assured that he is accepted by God." the second was "that the wicked who die without faith in

---

[3] See appendix p131 for copy of agreement.

[4] This was equivalent to an annual rent today of £72.50 with a £52 legal fee.

[5] Again this is not an insignificant sum, being about £194 in today's value.

Christ suffer never ending punishment.". I doubt many on trials would offer such sentiments today. The Quarterly Meeting itself took a decision which seems strict even for the time. It was agreed that no Sunday services should be given up for the purpose of attending funerals and choir members were also asked not to absent themselves for this purpose. Sunday funerals were brought about at this time because employers would not allow absence for this reason and repeated offence could bring about dismissal. The application of such a stricture on local preachers and choir members seems harsh.

CHAPTER THREE

A period of turmoil

The Revd William Bennett commenced superintendency in September 1887, he was already 64 but he was nonetheless asked to continue his ministry in Normanton in the following year. In September 1888, when he should have been starting his second year in office, a letter was sent to his wife, Elizabeth, with condolences on his passing. There was no retirement age at this time and ministers regularly worked until forced to retire owing to ill health, which was often earlier than might be assumed. A tablet was to be erected in Normanton Church in memory of Mr Bennett, although there is no memory of it today.

This introduced twelve months of struggle and sadness to the circuit. The replacement minister sent by the district was the Revd W B Luddington who was appointed at the September meeting. At the November meeting it was reported that he had been taken ill and he was given a fortnight's rest. Within days a letter of sympathy is sent to his mother and daughter. William Broadbent Luddington was only 45 years old, but had spent much of the previous fifteen years as a missionary in Fernando Po, now Bioko, which was a Spanish colony off the coast of West Africa from where he and his wife returned to Yorkshire in poor health. Mrs Luddington had died in the August, William surviving her only until the November. The administration of the meeting now fell on Richard Hall, the senior steward. It was decided to ask the district for permission for a preacher, Mr Eccles, to run the circuit until next July. This would be the time of the following Conference. The accounts show that Mr Eccles had been employed since Revd Luddington was taken ill and had been paid £9 for his services. The new proposal would have him living in the minister's house and be paid a salary of £22, an increase of £2 on that paid to Revd Luddington. This plan seems not to have been acceptable as the March meeting was presided over by the Revd Bartholomew Haddon, a young man, who was to remain in charge of the circuit, living in the minister's house until September when a new minister was appointed.

Perhaps because of Mr Haddon's inexperience, a controversial decision was taken at his first meeting. It was agreed that the society should be allowed to use fermented wine for sacraments. This was clearly going to cause a problem as the circuit had formed its branch of the Connexional Temperance Society in 1883 and there had been several disciplinary cases brought against members who had been known to abuse strong drink. Sure enough at the following meeting the matter was raised and the decision reversed.

The matter of Lee Brigg and an attempt to find a house to hold services there was raised again in the June meeting. This pretty much lost cause seems to have been brought to the fore again while they had an inexperienced minister to deal with. One of the first decisions taken under the new minister was to take Lee Brigg off the plan.

A busy circuit, a reducing membership

Mr Haddon's short spell in charge came to an end when, in September 1889, the Revd Alexander McKechnie was appointed as superintendent of the circuit. Preparations had been on going for some months as the circuit upgraded the furnishings in the Minister's house. A new spring mattress and several other household items were acquired, although this was still the rented property in The Grove. Alexander McKechnie was no youngster, an experienced minister of 68 years old who had been travelling for 48 years, quite a different kettle of fish from the young man the circuit had been dealing with for the last few months. The circuit did not part with Mr Haddon on bad terms, he was invited to preach during the following quarter and seems to have been well regarded.

An Early portrait of Alexander McKechnie

With the position of women, generally, in church office at this time it is worth noting that a Miss Hopkinson was invited to preach at New Sharlston in March 1890 and to follow that with a lecture on the Monday. Miss Hopkinson was one of a number of women mentioned during the early years as missioners and preachers. Despite this there were no women in circuit office in Normanton, either in the Primitive Circuit or in the Wesleyan Circuit based at Rothwell.

Another highlight of this year was the sending of a student to Manchester as a candidate for the ministry. The circuit meeting agreed to raise a subscription to support Richard Thompson at college.

From January until March an evangelist was employed to work in the circuit living half time at Normanton and half at New Sharlston. It was agreed that he should be paid £1 5s per week, although bed and board would have been provided.[6] There was legislation being brought forward at Conference for a new order of evangelists and the circuit voted to oppose this formalising of the situation.

---

[6] Despite the inclusion of board and lodgings, this was not a very generous wage by today's standards, being the equivalent of about £75

Relationships

Hope Town Church, Primitive, were in negotiation to join Castleford Circuit. Although Hope Town was not in Normanton at that time, and was within the Castleford Circuit boundaries as described in the recent discussion between the two circuits, it had been part of Pontefract Circuit until this point. The Church building had been in Foxbridge Row, Hopetown since 1870, but was now looking to move to Castleford Road. Normanton Circuit decided at the September 1890 meeting to await an approach by either party before entering any discussion. This seems to have been a wise decision as Hope Town came into the Normanton Circuit in 1901 as Castleford Road, thus moving the circuit boundary again.

During this same quarter, decisions were taken which suggest a continuing relationship with the Railway Servants. This was a mission organisation attached to the Railways which met within the stations and related directly to their employees. It was agreed that they should hold a camp meeting at Normanton in August 1891, not only for railway employees, but as an encouragement for the circuit. Also, in December, the Railway Servants were permitted to preach a sermon and take a collection in Normanton Church at the funeral of a Mr Taylor.

This was a period of growth in the circuit properties, if not in the congregations. Normanton Trustees were seeking a loan from Chapel Aid towards the cost of further development of the school building, Altofts applied to Chapel Aid for £160 for work on their church and there was considerable expenditure on the minister's house with new carpet, oil cloth for the floors and general decoration being undertaken. As Altofts (Lock Lane) carried out a continuing programme of development over the period, with new vestries and a school room being added to the church, it is difficult to say what the loan they sought was intended for, but there was more than sufficient work and local input to justify it.

Streethouse applied to the circuit for permission to buy a new organ. Perhaps because there was a history of financial struggle in this church the circuit's agreement was conditional on the congregation raising £35 of the £40 cost of the organ.

By the end of 1891 a decision was made to put the number of the preaching house in St John's Terrace on the plan (No. 53). Clearly this mission was now seen as a viable congregation needing regular appointments. Not everything was quite so positive; a proposal was brought that any preacher neglecting his appointments without a satisfactory reason should be suspended for a quarter. Clearly the stigma of suspension was a potent threat, a very different attitude to that of today. On several occasions over the years the minutes record preachers on trial who ask to withdraw only to have the circuit decline their resignation.

Having served three years on the Normanton station, Revd Alexander McKechnie applied for superannuation and the circuit signed the papers and agreed his departure. The Revd John Binns was invited and accepted the appointment. Mr Binns, and his wife Martha, were originally from Halifax and he had been a probationer in the Wakefield Circuit in but was stationed in Liskeard in Cornwall when he was invited. Although ministers were stationed in whatever part of the country needed them, there was a tendency for those who had served their early years away to seek to return to home territory. In a time when travel was not easy, this was not surprising and Mr Binns had family still living in Halifax.

When he arrived there were 391 members reported and it had been agreed to increase the minister's salary to £27 10s a quarter while at the same time the house rent had increased to £4 7s 9d per quarter. It is notable that his reception service was planned with invitations to the Baptist minister and the minister of the Independent Chapel, but not to the Wesleyan or United Methodist ministers of the town.

The members of Beckbridge Church and those appointed to preach there had to show a particular degree of commitment as the preachers were reminded on the plan to come early in time to commence Sunday School for the young and be prepared to stay all day with the adults, who would move into Sunday School mode after the morning service.

A Bad Year To Start a Ministry

1893 was a bad year for Yorkshire. There had been a series of disputes between the mine owners and the miners culminating in a wage cut of 25% made in the September. This led to a county wide strike and trouble at most of the pits. On September 17 there was a riot in Featherstone, the next large town, and two miners were shot by the soldiers called in to quell the trouble. Over the year the circuit membership declined steadily to a low of 343 at the height of the strike. Although the Circuit Minutes report that the "coal struggle has had a bad effect on the circuit", it does not make clear the cause of this decline. Some people would have been lost to the area, some, perhaps, disillusioned with the church and some unable to pay the dues necessary to maintain membership.

The listings of the officers of the various churches show few of these were miners. Even at the two Sharlston churches the majority of those who held office were tradesmen or self employed. Newspaper reports for the time suggest that sympathy for the strikers was not always strong in the wider community. Sadly there are no records to tell us how the churches behaved towards the struggling miners. John Binns was himself from a working class family, both his parents being mill workers, but there is nothing to say how he was able to engage with those involved.

There were now seven churches in the circuit if we include St John's, which was a preaching house. After the September 1894 meeting two stewards, R. Hall and T. Woodman were delegated to accompany the minister to Sharlston Common to discuss the deficiency with them. The problem was that each quarter the circuit accounts were laid before the meeting and the total deficit divided between the various churches. On this occasion Sharlston Common had not paid their share, nor offered a process to do so. The irony is that Richard Hall was one of the founding members of the endeavour there. Since this church was in a predominantly mining community this may well be the cause of the difficulty they face at this time.

In December it was another church which was facing difficulties. The circuit decided to sell Beckbridge Church, that is the wooden building, and to take responsibility for the deficit and the balance, any balance in the account to be transferred to the minister's house account. The cause in Beckbridge was not abandoned as it was agreed to find the use of a cottage for services. When we consider closing churches today it is perhaps interesting to note this struggle to maintain a congregation in Beckbridge. As can be seen from a map it was barely ten minutes walk from the main circuit church in Wakefield Road. In the event, there is clearly no surplus as Mr Binns was authorised to borrow £36 so that Mrs Emma Backer might receive the debt owed her for the church.

Mr Binns was succeeded in 1895 by the Revd John Teece, a minister in his early 40s with a wife and three sons. The presence of the children affected his remuneration, but there was not otherwise an increase in salary.

A scheme to employ a young man to help the minister in the winter months was entered into and a Mr W. E Walker from the Walkenden circuit was employed at £13 per quarter. He was to be housed in Sharlston. Perhaps of interest is that the preachers' meeting is mentioned this quarter for the first time. In previous times the duties of plan and preachers' duties and discipline had been dealt with by the ministers and stewards before the full meeting of the circuit. Revd Teece was elected as a delegate to the district meeting, this does not appear to be by right of his office.

Although the building had been sold, Beckbridge continued a presence on the plan. There was no mention of where they meet for services during this time. The circuit remained determined to maintain a presence here and nine members are transferred to Beckbridge from other societies in the circuit with the intention of improving the society. St John's had again disappeared from the plan but there still seem to have been intermittent services. A letter is sent to Mr J. Madeley thanking him for all his years of service in opening his house for services and his willingness to continue to do so until the Mission Room is ready. Subscriptions were sought for this project and by September 1897 there was a report on the erection of the Mission Room.

The September meeting in 1896 had re-invited Mr Teece and, perhaps more importantly, had made the decision to buy a minister's house. The house trustees were instructed to borrow £50 to pay a Mr Foster. There was a further £30 to be borrowed and along with £20 from reserves this was to be spent on furniture. No 39 Church Lane, Freeston Terrace, was to remain the Normanton manse till after Methodist Union became a reality in the area.

As I have mentioned previously, local preachers' resignations were often declined and a Mr Gordon, a preacher on trial, offered his resignation as he did not feel he was up to the task. The meeting declined to accept and, while sympathising with his discouragement, assured him that his services had always been acceptable. Since he went on full plan a year later, he seems to have accepted their verdict.

Sharlston Common were given permission to engage a Mrs Coulbeck of Grimsby for revival services in the June. This was followed by Normanton and Streethouse engaging her for a fortnight each later in the year. There was a strong tradition of women revival preachers amongst the Prims and these women are mentioned at intervals as they are brought into the circuit for specific periods. Although there was never any suggestion that these were deaconesses, the Wesley Deaconess Order was nominating Deaconess Evangelists who operated in a similar manner at about this time.

By June 1898 the reported membership was only 288:

Normanton	114
Altofts (Lock Lane)	44
St John's	6
New Sharlston	53
Streethouse	14
Sharlston Common	38
Beckbridge	19

Although I have been unable to find any sources to confirm this, it would seem that the troubles in the coal industry were the likely root of this sudden collapse in membership. New Sharlston in particular had suffered particular loss, being reduced to half the membership it had reached in 1888.

In September 1898 a new minister was appointed to the circuit, the Revd John Bennett a man in his early 40s who had served around Yorkshire most of his ministry and was married with two sons. The welcome service planned for Mr Bennett included a much wider invitation than previously and was to include the ministers of all the Non-Conformist churches in the town. The state of the circuit was perhaps reflected in the fact that each society was asked to provide some aid towards the renovation of the house, a cost which had normally been voted from circuit funds. The minister was allowed discretion in the supply of "sundries", those small items necessary to a household, and was allowed £1 a quarter for this expense.

A further example of improved relationships with the Wesleyans was to come within a very short time after the minister's arrival. For about a year the Wesleyan church in Wakefield Road had been engaged in Mission and were now considering St John's as an area of possible expansion. As can be seen from the table on the previous page the mission work of the Primitive Methodist Circuit in this area was struggling and, although there had been regular discussions in regard to the building of a mission room in the estate, this had not reached fruition. Mr Bennett received a letter from Revd John Tyreman, the Wesleyan minister in December 1898:

Dear Mr Bennett,
    I am writing at the instance of our Leader's Meeting to lay before you its view on a matter in which you with us are deeply interested.
    For some time we have felt that there are parts of our town - notable St John's and the outlying borders of Woodhouse - that are in a destitute spiritual condition; and the people in them are very inadequately cared for. We have also felt that we are doing too little ourselves of earnest mission work among the masses, who seem not only outside all the churches, but outside our thoughts and prayers and beyond our influence.
    We do not forget that you already in St John's, (sic) and have labored there with the best of your ability for many years. Upon such rights and possessions we could not encroach without at least a material and cordial understanding. We still believe however, that in so great a population religious work is possible of greater development than at present, and if you can extend, revive, and build up your cause there we shall most heartily rejoice in that fact and wish you God-speed.
    My purpose therefore in bringing the matter before you, is not to ask for anything, nor even to sketch any policy that we may entertain, but simply to inform you of our desire to move in the direction I have indicated and to be assured that between us, (two sister Methodist churches) there will be no clashing of interests, and no disturbance of a feeling of mutual goodwill.

I may say again that we do not believe in entering the sphere
of work an influence belonging to any church -   especially one
so closely allied with us, and as identical in its spirit and
methods - unless there is an urgent necessity and work we can
take up that no other church is doing.

If you can bring this matter before your Quarterly Meeting, we
shall feel freer to take such steps as the necessity of the case
may require and be able we hope to avoid both overlapping and
any appearance of alienation or competition in our work.

Wishing you every success and joy in your work. Believe me.

Yours very sincerely

John T. Tyerman

The immediate response to this from the Primitive meeting
was to resolve that the work at St John's be discontinued
and the Wesleyan minister be informed of that decision. The
alacrity of that decision is surprising since the work at St
John's had appeared on the business of the Quarterly
Meeting regularly for some years and there seemed to be a
commitment to the erection of some form of mission
building. That the circuit gave up this ambition must have
been a disappointment to those few who had struggled
valiantly in the cause over many years, not least John
Madeley who had put his house at the disposal of the circuit
during all that time. The St John's Terrace Committee
requested that £10 be granted to Streethouse and £6 to
Beckbridge. This was approved by the Circuit and the
account was wound up.

Perhaps it should be noted that despite the apparent
connection with the arrival of John Bennett, the decision
regarding St John's was a matter for the laity, not the
minister, just as the drive to take this up by the Wesleyans
was led by the lay people from their church. There was a very
clear understanding of the superintendent's representative
role in the relationship between the minister and the
Leaders' Meeting. A further example of this was the
instruction to the superintendent to appeal from the pulpit

for Sunday School workers at both Sharlston Common and New Sharlston.

This last year of the Nineteenth century continued to show a decrease in membership and the circuit recorded a decrease of 10 over the year.

CHAPTER FOUR

Into the Twentieth Century

The new century opened with a question of church union. The Quarterly Meeting was asked to discuss and vote on union with the Bible Christians, a Methodist sect based largely in Cornwall and Devon. This proposal was rejected by the meeting which would seem to have reflected the view of the Primitive Methodist Church nationally as no such union took place.

Perhaps with a spirit of optimism, or from a sense of the need for new mission, six camp meetings were planned and dates fixed to hold them in the locality of each of the churches.

The minister's house was still a financial burden which had not been budgeted for in the long term and there were various efforts made to assist in this. One unusual effort was that of Mr and Mrs Chapman who gave a circuit tea to celebrate their silver wedding and donated the proceeds to the minister's house fund. Because most of the monies needed to finance manses came from District Housing funds, there was not the same risk as borrowing from the bank. The cost of providing housing was always a difficulty which seemed to drag on beyond good management in some cases.

The minister's salary was raised to £30, although this was of less benefit to Mr Bennett as the circuit was no longer paying a child's allowance and he still had one boy of school age.

The December meeting agreed, what was doubtless Connexional policy, that all new candidates for local preaching should take their examinations in three parts:

1. Theology and History of Connexion.
2. Grammar and the Life of Christ.
3. Consolidated Minutes and General subjects.

Clearly six subjects and a quite broad educational requirement. Many of these preachers were working men, colliers and railway workers and this reflects both the commitment needed and the opportunity for wider education made available through their church connection. Most of the organisers in the local mining union came from the churches and some of them preachers.

The service times were jealously guarded as times of preaching. New Sharlston was given permission to give a "service of song" on Sunday December 23 but it was decided that a notice should be put on the plan to say that in future no "service of song" should be given on a Sunday evening.

The circuit started 1901 with continuing optimism as they looked forward to appointing a new superintendent in the next year and a discussion took place as to the possible appointment of an evangelist to work alongside him.

Beckbridge applied for permission to buy land, and this was approved allowing them to raise funds for a new church. Streethouse, too, was raising funds but for a new organ.

In the summer the circuit appointed mission bands to be led by two women of the membership to conduct mission services and evangelistic work in the smaller churches. The offer of the use of a missionary van from the Connexion was accepted in July and it was decided that it should be used in Normanton, Altofts, Beckbridge and New Sharlston over a period of four weeks. Clearly Beckbridge had bounced back from the doldrums.

Another boost was received at this time. Hopetown Primitive Methodist Church had been, for a few years, part of the Castleford Circuit and situated in Foxbridge Row on the edge of Normanton Common. In 1897 the strong society there built a new church and school in Castleford Road and now they applied to transfer to the Normanton circuit. This was accepted with the agreement of Castleford and the transfer papers for the Society and Trust were signed in July 1901. This required a payment to the Connexional and

District Equalization Fund of the proportions due on 75 members. Normanton had grown by 25% in one leap.

With the confirmation that Revd W. R. Fallas was to be stationed in Normanton from July 1902 the circuit places an advert in the Primitive Methodist World for a "Hired Local Preacher". Twenty applications were received for the post and it was decided to interview six of these. A Mr Frudd was offered the post at the £15 salary he requested and the circuit stewards are tasked with finding him a home in Beckbridge. Other than preaching, his duties were to include visiting at the places appointed in the afternoon. Mr Frudd did not seem to have been a great success, as within a quarter, Mr Starling had been employed to supply his work and the June meeting decided to remove Mr Frudd from the plan as he had left the station. Mr Starling, who had been lodged with a Mr Creamer, was asked to stay until the end of July when an advertisement was to be placed for a new Hired Local Preacher. No indication was given as to why Mr Starling should not be invited to fulfil the role.

The Revd William Reacher Fallas and his wife Fanny move from Bramley to Normanton into a volatile circuit with several areas of tension. The Hired Local Preacher problem rumbled on for some time and the new militancy regarding Teetotalism must have created some difficulties as the circuit now added a note on the plan to read "We strongly urge all members, official and unofficial, to entirely abstain from intoxicating liquors." At Streethouse there was long term strife and dissension which revolved around personal relationships. This matter had been before the Circuit Meeting, referred to the District and still there was no resolution. Now the Circuit Meeting resolved that the Superintendent should be empowered to deal with the matter "as best in his judgement". The dispute seems to have centred around a remark by a Mr Butterfield, a local preacher and member at Streethouse, which had caused severe offence to the congregation. Although he had made some attempt to apologise and insisted he had meant no harm this had continued for several years and was still unresolved when William Fallas was appointed.

New Trustees

Beckbridge had its plans for a new building approved and Normanton is looking to buy a plot of land adjoining the church and school. At Normanton only two of the original Trust members, Benjamin Pipe and Benjamin Walmsley were still willing and able to serve, so that a new trust was formed. The new Trustees are named as:

Isaac Taylor, wheat importer; Richard Hall, joiner; Daniel Thomas Woodman, boot and shoe maker; Francis Chapman, engine driver; Joseph Underwood, grocer; Benjamin Taylor, grocer; George Taylor, grocer; William Henry Morgan, Thomas Wilkinson, grocer; Robert Thompson, horsekeeper; John Edwin Smith, fruiterer; George Rutherford, railway inspector; Daniel Lister, engine tenter; Charles Bickerdyke, engine tenter; Thomas Gordon, engine tenter[7].

All men, and mostly shopkeepers. The two railwaymen were both from the upper echelons of employment in the railway, one of the largest employers in the area. The last three named did work in the mining industry, but they were engineers not colliers.

The plans for Beckbridge were going forward rapidly and it was agreed that Beckbridge Society should raise £450 towards the total £1050 cost of the building. The circuit agreed to pay the interest on a further £500 for six years. The source of the remaining £100 is not recorded in the circuit report. These two churches and Castleford Road are

---

[7] The term "engine tenter" was common in the north of England and in Scotland and was applied particularly to those who worked the winding engines in the mines. Such men would be skilled, responsible for the maintenance as well as the running of the engines.

to be placed at the top of the plan and bracketed together as Normanton Societies. Unfortunately there is no explanation as to the rationale for this decision but, although it seems to present opportunity for division, there is never any recorded resentment from the other four societies.

Over the years there had been occasional problems reported of local preachers who had been disciplined for some indiscretion involving alcohol, but now the Circuit Meeting took a very firm stand and required that "none but abstainers may be local preachers". A notice to that effect is put on the plan. This rule was applied to the new applicant for the post of Hired Local Preacher. Provided he was a total abstainer, Mr Coulson was offered the post from July 30th at £1 5s per week.

A decision was taken by the circuit meeting that sacraments were to be performed as requested by the leaders' meeting. This bald statement in the minutes is unexplained. When the circuit was formed, sacraments were to be held in each preaching place once a month. Whether this practice had slipped or a different view of the sacrament now pertained cannot be ascertained. One clue might be in the later decision that baptisms should be held on Sunday mornings, afternoons and weekday evenings. This move away from solely Sunday services suggests a change in the theological understanding around this service. Shortly after this decision was taken a Mr Dodd, a local preacher,was accused of Sunday Trading and after coming before a preachers' meeting he was dropped from the plan. There would seem to be a different mood in the circuit leadership than in the nineteenth century.

The circuit staffing continues to be somewhat erratic and a new Hired Local Preacher was appointed, this time to be based at New Sharlston. The new man was a Mr Escott and he remained with the circuit until they call out[8] a young minister called James Palmer. James was 27 but still single, which was part of the criteria for probation. The minutes do not refer to him as Reverend in his first two years although he receives repeat invitations. The salary he received was exactly the same as the Hired Local Preacher, £16 per quarter, and he would have been lodged with a member of the congregation. Mr Escott left the service of the circuit on this appointment "to seek greater opportunities for ministerial work" and joined the Congregational church. He seems not to have been successful in his ambitions as he returned to the Prims as a local preacher after two years.

In October of 1904, a special event was planned in the town, a Teacher's Conference (Sunday School) with a public meeting in the evening and a tea. The invited preacher for the day was, the Revd Flenshaw, and at the evening event there were to be two ministers and a choir. 1000 handbills were printed and distributed for this event which must have covered most houses in the town. The cost of would be covered by a charge of sixpence for the tea.

Lee Brigg still exercised the minds of the circuit leadership and in March 1905 the ministers and circuit stewards were asked to look at the possibility of a mission there. Looking at this concern from the perspective of the twenty first century, it is difficult to understand why so much time was given to it. Perhaps it was the distance between Wakefield Road church and Lock Lane. This was not open countryside, but a long ribbon of housing, a community without a church within it, which may have seemed like a barrier between the Normanton churches and the Altofts church. What is noticeable is that there is little mention of Lock Lane in the

---

[8] This seems to be the term used when appointing a probationary minister for the first time.

Circuit Minutes and its independence may have created a desire to close the distance.

At this Quarterly Meeting there was a proposal to change the name of Beckbridge to Park Side if the society approved. There was clearly no approval as it kept its original name until closure.

In September 1905, Revd Fallas returned to Bramley and Thomas Dickinson was appointed Superintendent. James Palmer was invited for a third year and his salary increased to £18. He is now referred to as Reverend, although his probation was not completed until 1908. James Palmer's time with the circuit was not without event as in October 1906 his attention was drawn to the neglect of an appointment at Hope Town and a request from Castleford Road[9], that he not be planned there was accepted at the same meeting.

Mr Dickinson was a married man of about 50 and he and his wife were accompanied by their nineteen year old son and a servant. Few of the ministers stationed in Normanton had live-in servants but it was not uncommon at this time.

It was decided to start a circuit magazine with Revd Dickinson appointed editor. The first issue was intended to have a circulation of 400, as there were now reckoned to be 410 members in the circuit. The *Home Messenger* as it was titled, was produced in October 1906 and the covers were sold as advertising with the intention of an increased circulation of 1000 copies. This was a very short lived venture, as it was discontinued in February 1907 owing to lack of advertising revenue.

The circuit was pleased to have produced another candidate for the ministry, a Mr Rowley had passed his exam for admittance as a candidate and the circuit approved his

---

[9] Despite the confusion of names at this point these are in fact, the same church.

application for the Lamb scholarship. Not everyone was prepared to go through the Methodist candidating process and another local preacher leaves to join the Congregational church, with a view to ministry.

The trustees of the minister's house were to meet with a view to reducing the debt. It was not always easy to see this cost in the accounts as it appears as rent. When the circuit received another accredited minister in 1908, this time a married man, a second house at 356 Castleford Road is shown with a rent payment.[10]

Revd Palmer was due to leave in September 1908 and, as a precursor of his being stationed, he was required to go on the approved list. A copy of his journal and sermons were sent to the District and the Connexion for approval.

As the ministers change again, the membership numbers are agreed but the Streethouse returns still show the presence of discord, as there were a number of entries against which there was a query.

Two new ministers

From September 1908 the circuit had a complete change of staff, Philip Thornton Yarker, a 63 year old, came as superintendent. He and his wife, Emma were accompanied by three of their four children, young men in their early twenties. The second minister was a "young man", William Woodley, who was to live at 365 Castleford Road, close to Castleford Road and Beckbridge churches. Although William arrived as a single man he was married shortly thereafter and was to have two children during his time in Normanton and while his salary was £5 less than the superintendent's,

---

[10] This second house was always a rented property. The term "house rent" in the minutes covered both direct rent paid to a landlord and a sum set aside by the circuit to repay the loan or interest on a loan for a property they had bought.

the children's allowance would increase that to nearly the same amount.

Although Philip Yarker remained in Normanton until 1912, his eldest son, a local preacher on the plan, left the circuit a year earlier.

In March 1912 50 members were taken off the Circuit roll of these 26 were removals. Most of the removals were miners from Castleford Road Church who had transferred to Woodlesford Colliery from the Dom Pedro mine in Hopetown. This probably brought about the rationalisation listed at this time. Included amongst the removals were three members who had died, one who had moved to the Baptists and three to the Anglicans. Of more consequence were the others, four are simply listed as left, one member was suspended and twelve were listed as fallen. As can be seen from the detailed list of causes, these last would not have been voluntary removals, but those who had been excluded from their church for cause. Such cause could be a wide range of offences from consistently neglecting the means of grace to a variety of offences against the abstention rulings which the circuit operated at this time.

The circuit meeting adopted a training regime for Local Preachers and exhorters that required them to sit half yearly examinations during their period on trial with examinations in theology, homiletics, biblical introduction, PM polity, Christian evidence and English grammar. Passes in each of these subjects were required if the preacher was to progress to the next stage of their training.

In 1912 two new ministers replaced Yarker and Woodley, although they were both only to remain for two years. Thomas H Bryant who was married with one child, came as Superintendent and the second minister was Edgar Reavley, a single man of 28. If the record of Methodist ministers is an indicator, men did not marry young at this period.

Lock Lane was in the awkward situation that half of its trustees had died and the other half were ready to retire. It seems that such situations more usually came to light with the arrival of a new superintendent. In March 1913 sixteen new trustees were appointed. Since the membership had not recently been more than about 25 this would have accounted for most of the members, and since there is, as yet, no indication of women in such offices, perhaps all those eligible.

In December of that year Sharlston Common trustees were given permission to sell the old wooden chapel which had served them for 24 years as they completed the new church in Weeland Road which was to remain in use until they closed in 1980.

One unusual aspect of this meeting was that the circuit finances showed a deficit of £10 owing to the ministers. This deficit was allocated to all of the churches, but a failure to be able to pay the ministers was a serious situation.

On paper this was quite a strong circuit. The circuits income from churches should have been £75 per quarter, in excess of that needed to cover the minister's salaries. There were 357 members in the seven churches and a strong group of society and circuit stewards. The circuit could boast 19 local preachers and two exhorters and a nine person mission band. This should not have been a struggling circuit. Of the seven churches, only three, Wakefield Road, Castleford Road and Altofts were registered for the solemnization of marriages. The plan notes that baptisms would be administered at Sunday morning and Weekday evening services, this would not have required the presence of a minister but was the responsibility of the Society Steward to arrange.

There is no indication in the minutes of the Quarterly Meetings why both ministers were released after two years, but this could have nothing to do with the coincidental start of the First World War in August 1914 as invitations were not issued to the two incumbents in 1913. Whatever lay behind this abrupt change, two new ministers were appointed to the circuit in September 1914 and in December it was decided to ask them to remain until 1918.

Revd. William Tonks came to the circuit at the age of 46, a married man with a family of 4 children, although the eldest of these was 18 and probably did not come to Normanton with the rest of the family. They were to stay for five years, the longest any minister had remained in the station up to that time. His colleague, Revd William R Reed does not appear in any records I have been able to find, but he would have been younger. He certainly had no children as he was not paid an allowance, and may not have been married,

These two were coming into the circuit at a time of worry for many. War had broken out, and although optimism was still the mood as was evidenced by a resolution of the circuit meeting of September 1915 authorising the ministers to hold a thanksgiving service if peace was declared in the following quarter, many of the young men of the circuit were away in the services.

From the end of the year the plans were to carry the names of those young men and prayers were to be offered for their safekeeping.

The circuit sent a recommendation to the District Synod asking that the salary for probationers should not be less than £20 and that for authorised ministers be not less than £30. Demonstrating their commitment to this belief, Normanton raised the salary of the Superintendent to £35 and that of the second minister to £30.

March 1916 noted the retirement from the Circuit House Trustees of Richard Hall. Mr Hall was a significant presence in Primitive Methodism in the Normanton area over many years. He had come to the area as a foreman joiner at the Sharlston colliery and was instrumental in founding the society and church there. He served as choirmaster at Sharlston, Altofts and Normanton at various times and was a circuit officer for nearly fifty years. In 1889 he left the colliery to set up in Normanton as a joiner and undertaker, continuing to serve the circuit until his death in 1919.

The same meeting granted leave of absence to Revd Reed who had experienced a call to army and naval chaplaincy. This never seems to have been fulfilled as he remains involved in the circuit until 1918. In 1917 the circuit had made "A special case for stationing" for the invitation of both ministers for a fourth year. Having made this case they then proceeded to invite both ministers for a fifth year. Revd Tonks accepted this invitation and Revd Reed declined.

It was at this 1917 meeting that we find the first mention of a female local preacher. A Miss Liversedge had her credentials received and was placed on full plan.

The meeting petitioned the government to prohibit the sale of strong drink for the duration of the war and for six months thereafter. Unfortunately there is no record of what prompted this action and clearly it was not successful.

By the August meeting there were several concerns to be seen. It was resolved to send out a circular letter to all 381 members in the circuit appealing to them "to use every endeavour in attending the Means of Grace on Sundays and weekdays. Such an action would suggest real concern regarding the spiritual health of the circuit. At the same time the finance committee minutes show regular deficits in the giving of the societies. A little over a year before, it had been proposed to invite both ministers to continue for another year. This meeting resolved to dissolve the invitation committee formed at the May meeting and "that steps be taken to secure absolute relief from a second minister". From this and further minutes it would seem that a circuit became a two minister station by consent of Conference and could not simply cease to invite ministers off their own accord. This decision was to prove a little difficult to have approved.

The cost of the houses continues to rise. The circuit manse "rent" is increased to £7 and the actual rent of the house for the second minister rises to £5.

Despite these problems the circuit clearly tried to act honourably and award both ministers a £5 war bonus as well as paying an allowance of £2 10s, for there being an extra week in the final quarter of the year[11]. It was also agreed to keep on the second house if Mr Reed was called to chaplaincy. This action helped to confuse the understanding of the Connexional Committee considering the matter of relief from a second minister.

The meeting decided to send a letter to Mr Bloomfield of New Sharlston "commending his splendid devotion to our church there". This was the third such letter sent to Mr and Mrs Bloomfield in this regard.

From March to June 1918 considerable discussion took place about the second minister and the rented house. Nothing is stated but it seems as though there is some unrest about the ministry of Mr Reed and his name never appears again in the circuit minutes. Although the list of ministers in the 1942 Centenary Souvenir booklet shows William Reed serving until 1919 the second house is empty from March 1918 and the superintendent's salary is raised to £40 with no mention of a payment to Mr Reed. The second house was the property of a Mrs Leach and the circuit struggled to pay her what was owed in rent to finalise the lease.

Further evidence of the dissatisfaction with Revd Reed appears in the June minutes where we read: "A resolution re the ministry of Revd W R Reed in this circuit during the past 4 years be drawn up by No 1 (the Superintendent) and circuit stewards and be placed on record.". This is followed by a note that Revd W. C. Tonks be asked to release himself from his present war-time commercial employment so that he may devote his whole time to ministerial duties.

---

[11] This would support my understanding from the terminology used that minister's payments were seen as a salary rather in terms of a stipend.

Unfortunately there had been no mention of these duties previously.

It was further suggested at the June meeting that the circuit house should be replenished from the furnishings of the second house. The minutes record, not only that Mr Tonks protested at this, but that he insisted on signing a note in the minute to record his protest. This seems to have been a successful ploy and the house was refurbished at a cost of £9 7s 2d. Despite the clear evidence of cash problems the Superintendent's salary was again increased in September to £45

With no house rent to pay, the manse[12] committee was granted £30 per year for debt reduction. It is agreed to pay £70 off the mortgage and to seek a loan of £250 from Chapel Aid.

To my surprise it is only at this time that it was decided that every society should keep a baptism register, although there are several older copies in the Wakefield archives. Additionally it is agreed to give baptism certificates at every baptism at a charge of sevenpence.

Beyond the Great War

With the war at last at an end plans were made for a Great United Thanksgiving Service at Wakefield Road Church on January 15th 1919. The language used differs from the first suggestion for such a service. This is about the end of the war; in 1915 they still hoped for a declaration of peace.

All the churches were asked to work towards the formation of "A League of Nations". From this and several of the other resolutions the circuit had passed previously, it can be seen that it was taken for granted that local churches

---

[12] This is the first use of "manse" in any of the records although I think this may simply be the personal usage of the secretary at this time.

and ordinary people had a role to play in national and international affairs.

It was again resolved to pay a special war grant to the minister. This time it is decided to pay him £50 which is to be raised by a levy of 3d per member over a period of ten weeks. There is no explanation as to why it is felt proper to make these grants.

There are now more women appearing on the plan and two are mentioned as exhorters on the latest plan.

A letter from the connexion was received before the March meeting regarding the "relief" from a second minister which indicates some confusion in understandings. The circuit had requested and gained the support of the 1918 District Synod for a permanent relief from a second minister. The Conference appears not to have acknowledged this and treated the request as of a temporary nature. Assuming the request granted, the circuit had disposed of the house and the furniture. Connexion was clearly unhappy about this state of affairs, but eventually agreed to accept the situation. Perhaps because he was being paid above the connexional rate for a superintendent, Mr Tonks' salary is listed in the accounts as salary plus bonus, although this could indicate an intent that it should not be an expectation for his successor. If this were so it seems not to have held sway as September brought a new superintendent, the Revd John E. Leuty, who was to be paid £52 10s, quite an increase of that paid to Mr Tonks. Revd Leuty, aged 64, was a minister with twenty years service behind him. His wife also has her credentials received and her name placed on the plan as a local preacher, one of a growing band of women since the commencement of the war. The accounts record the expenditure of £4 16s 6d on renovations to the manse in time for the new minister taking possession.

The saga of the "relief" continued at the December Quarterly Meeting as a resolution was passed to say that the circuit could not see their way to pay the £2 10s per quarter demanded by the Connexion as a levy on the relief from a second minister. Since the circuit could clearly have found this sum, this decision is more a matter of rebellion against the system than hardship.

A rather sad note appears in the minutes of the Preacher's Meetings during this time. Mr Rowland Hall, who has served in the Royal Navy throughout the war, but whose name had remained on the plan, requested that he be allowed to resign. In December it was decided that his name should remain on the plan and that he should be seen by the minister about taking services again. His resignation is noted in the next quarter. Perhaps his faith was a casualty of war as happened to so many.

Early in 1920 an effort is made to decrease the debt on the manse and the payments were increased from £7 10s to £12 10s. As this was a quarterly payment it would still take some years to make a real difference to the amount owing.

In September the minister's salary was raised to £65 per quarter, £2 10s above the Connexional minimum. The levy for relief was now being paid although there is no decision entered in the minutes.

Two more preachers passed their connexional exams in the following June, Mrs J. Seymour who has passed with credit and Mr Harold Shiel. An ordination service was planned for both on a Sunday Evening.

Mr Leuty was invited for a fifth year and accepts conditionally.

The circuit was still enrolling members for the League of Nations Association, clearly this was something which had been successful in circuit life.

Mr Leuty came to the March 1922 Quarterly Meeting with the news that he intended to seek superannuation in 1923. His earlier conditional acceptance had been because his health was not robust and he had now made a decision to retire at the next Conference. Revd Leuty would be 69 by the time he became a supernumerary. Although ministers did seem to be asked to work longer than now, it was not unusual, as can be seen from this circuit's history, for health to bring their ministry to a close.

This meeting was notable also in that a new Church Committee was approved for Beckbridge Church which included five women in its twelve person membership.

Mr Stanley Oakley, who had completed his Local Preacher's examinations in 1921 was now candidating for the ministry and the September Circuit Meeting commended him to the district. Methodist Union is discussed for the first time and the meeting agrees resolutions on several points in the proposals. They did not approve of the supremacy of Ministerial Conference in matters ministerial, wishing this to rest with Representative session. On Doctrine: they requested that some statement of doctrine be drawn up based upon the Divine Revelation recorded in the Holy Scriptures alone as the supreme rule of faith and practice. This was in opposition to the proposal regarding Wesley's notes and sermons. They also required that authorisation of persons to administer the Sacraments be left in the hands of the Quarterly Meeting.

In March there was disappointment for Mr Oakley in that

Rev John Clague

his first attempt at the oral exam as a candidate for ministry was unsuccessful and the Circuit Meeting expressed its regret and encouraged him to try again.

Streethouse made a request to buy a new American organ and the Circuit gave permission if the church felt this was necessary.

Since Revd Leuty was leaving after Conference and a new minister, the Revd John N. Clague was appointed to the circuit, the house committee met to report on the state of the manse. Recommendations were made to paint and decorate the whole house, but in particular the main bedroom. It was recommended that the bedstead and mattress should also be replaced. The bed was supplied, but the decoration of the manse was deferred.

Revd John Nelson Clague came into the circuit at 43 years of age, accompanied by his wife Frances and one young son, their older boy having died four years previously. John had been eighteen years in the ministry and had served much of his time in Yorkshire.

The March meeting also gave permission to solicit subscriptions which would be a present to Stanley Oakley if he entered Hartley College. A year later there were further efforts to fund Stanley through college, but then no more mention of his endeavours in the following minutes. Stanley had been twenty-three when he candidated, the son of a miner, deputy overman, living in Castleford Road and he must have found it a struggle.

In the summer of 1924, Wakefield Road celebrated its jubilee with special services and musical events. Castleford Road were able to complete their new organ and Streethouse gained approval for their plans to build a new school at the rear of the church at a cost of £1,100. Streethouse was also given approval to apply to the District Building Fund for a loan of £500 towards this project.

Methodist Union again came before the Circuit Meeting in September 1924. The meeting was asked to vote on the question: "Are you in favour of the organic union of the Wesleyan Methodist, the Primitive Methodist and the United Methodist Churches on the basis of the scheme now submitted?" Of the 25 members present, four voted for and twenty against. It was to be another five years before further movement in this process took form.

The January meeting deliberated at length on invitations for a new superintendent from 1926 and they were eventually accepted by The Revd J. T. Clarke (I wonder how he felt looking back in the minutes to find that he was number ten in preference.).

One of the founding members of the Primitive Methodist Circuit in Normanton, Mr Benjamin Pipe had died at 78 years old. His name is one of those on the stones at the church although he had moved back to Derbyshire, where he was born, some years before. The Quarterly Meeting sent a letter of sympathy to his family, some of whom still lived in Normanton.

New Sharlston moved into a period of difficulty and unrest. There had been some problems in relation to both the Sunday School and the Church which resulted in the Sunday School Superintendent being removed from office. This was in relation to fundraising for renovations in the previous year. Mr Bloomfield was called in again to act as Assistant Sunday School Superintendent. In 1924 the Society had had twenty two members this was now down to fifteen and by 1929 it was to reduce to only nine.

Mr. J. Bloomfield

The circuit had always had a strong Sunday School tradition, with schools in most of the churches. In 1926 a meeting took place to arrange the union of the Sunday School work and Christian Endeavour under one organisation within the circuit. This new grouping continued in being until at least union in 1947.

At the end of the year the circuit stewards agree to buy new bedding for the minister's house to consist of one pair of blankets, one pair of sheets and a counterpane. There were also some new carpets and the cost is £25 13s.

The exterior of the manse was also in need of renovation and these costs brought about a decision not to make any repayment to the Chapel Aid Association for that month.

The Streethouse Trustees were given permission to renovate the church and thanks are recorded to Mr Charles Mounty for his generous gift of £50. Mr Mounty was a grocer from Whinney Lane who had, with his family, been active in the church since its early days.

The year ended with the recording of the death of another founding member, Mr W. H. Brown who had been a local preacher for 40 years and a Sunday School teacher at

Mr Charles Mounty

Wakefield Road church. He had also served as local secretary of the local League of Nations Union.

At this time the Preachers Meeting notes the resignation of Mr. Holcroft who, after 40 years service, had decided he had to join another communion. There is no mention of which, or of his reasons, but this would have been as the talks on union grew more positive.

The minutes of September 1926 record an allocation for the circuit funds of 5s 9d per member per quarter. This comes at a time when there were 344 members as well as seventeen on trial. The on trials would not count in the allocation and it is notable that there had been no mention of on trial members for some years, but with the appearance of the allocation based on members, the number jumped into prominence and remained so for the next decade.

Two Streethouse members rose to prominence as Mr W Seymour was appointed as Society Steward and his wife completed her Local Preachers exams. The circuit set a

Sunday evening service at Streethouse for her ordination service.

At the beginning of 1927 Beckbridge Church requested that a room at the rear of the Church, which can still be seen today, was designated as a school to which the circuit gave its agreement. There seems to be a constant renewal of buildings and property throughout the circuit. Castleford Road trustees asked the circuit for a grant in aid of debt reduction to help pay off the work they had been doing and this was granted, with £25 being given from circuit funds to clear the debt.

Revd John Clarke was invited to continue in the circuit until 1929 and, despite the problems he was facing, agreed to do so. First amongst these problems was to lead a deputation of circuit stewards to meet with the colliery officials at New Sharlston to ask for assistance with repairing and renovating the chapel there. This was the building erected by the Colliery Company and ceded to the Primitive Methodist Circuit by vote of those worshipping there. It is probable that the actual premises were still in the ownership of the company rather than the church which would have given the circuit some reason to go to them with their needs, but it was a delicate situation.

The manse in Church Lane (Freeston Terrace) continued to receive updating and renovation. In June a new kitchen range was installed at a cost of £15 10s.

There had been some disquiet expressed at a number of meetings about the credentials of preachers from outside the circuit occupying Methodist pulpits and now a long conversation took place at the Quarterly Meeting about what was seen as the growing custom of stewards inviting unauthorised persons to preach. There seemed also to be a problem with some local preachers sending unaccredited supplies when they were unable to fulfil their plan appointments. Great dissatisfaction was expressed with what was regarded as a dangerous practice.

The September meeting examined two candidates for the ministry. Mr William Hirst Baugh, the son of a Normanton miner, was approved as a candidate and his application for a scholarship to Hartley College is accepted. The voting was 20 for and 8 against. Mr John Stanley Clarke, the 26 year old son of the Minister was also approved but with a vote of 22 for none against, although such a figure would indicate six neutral.

The renovations at New Sharlston werere again raised and there is a measure of urgency. A meeting was to be arranged with Mr Fidler from the Colliery Company and the Minister and his colleagues.

Castleford Road had not yet received a decision regarding the loan requested and the meeting was urged to press the General Chapel Fund on this matter.

At Wakefield Road two young men, unnamed, had been renovating the vestries and the cellars of the Church and raising the funds to pay for the work themselves. Congratulations from the Quarterly Meeting are sent to them.

William Baugh was congratulated on passing his oral examination and the Quarterly Meeting wished him all success at synod, his next stage in candidating.

The minutes here contain what may well be an odd coincidence. A Mr H. Escott had resigned from the church and as a local preacher with the intention of of candidating for the Congregational ministry at Pontefract. A Mr T. E. Escott did exactly this in 1904, but subsequently returned to the Primitive Methodist Church. I can find no connection between the two persons.

The Altofts Church (Lock Lane) had been revalued for insurance purposes, clearly not before time, as the valuation was to be increased from £800 to £1800.

The year ended with the re-invitation of Mr Clarke, he was asked to remain until 1930 and he accepted. His wife, Sarah, was to have her name included in the list of auxiliary preachers.

Although 1928 opened with some good news from Castleford Road (they had managed to reduce their property debt by £302 10s to only £281 19s 8d with the aid of three very generous gifts from church members), things were not all so rosy. The May minutes were taken up to a great extent with an account of a long and protracted disagreement between two of the members of Wakefield Road. This problem largely centred around the choir and there are accusations going back as much as 30 years. Neither the Society Stewards, nor the minister have been able to bring this to any conclusion and the meeting refered the matter to a District Committee.

At Streethouse, Charles Mounty who was now 80 years old had asked to retire as Society Steward, a position he had held for 50 years. The Quarterly Meeting proposed that his name remain as a steward and Charles consented to this, although this was to be an honorary position.

The June meeting authorised the minister to meet with the Ladies' Bright Hour at New Sharlston to inform them that the minister must be present at the Annual General Meeting of the Bright Hour and all kindred organisations, and that their officials must be submitted to the Quarterly Meeting for confirmation. This resulted in a letter from the New Sharlston Bright Hour to the Quarterly Meeting protesting. The reply informed them that the organisation was Connexional and that all monies belonged to the Connexion and in the case of officers leaving all such monies should be handed over to the representatives of the organisation.

This dispute seemed to spell the end of the organisation at New Sharlston, but brought about a reorganisation in the Bright Hour within the Circuit. It was decided that the Bright Hours at Wakefield Road and Altofts should have a Class Book to which the names of members could be transferred, which would bring them into a more formal relationship with the church. Attendance and all class money should be recorded by the President of Bright Hour. The President should have a seat on both the Leaders' Meeting and the Quarterly Meeting. All similar organisations were to be asked to conform to this resolution.

At the opening of 1929 we hear of further losses amongst the founding fathers of the circuit. Mr Joseph Underwood of Wakefield Road was moving to Bishop Auckland after 50 years as a local preacher and having held every office in Wakefield Road as well as serving as a Circuit Steward. Presumably Mr Underwood was retiring and moving to live with family. Mr Charles Mounty from Streethouse, on the other hand, had passed away, and his death was reported to the circuit with deep regret.

At New Sharlston there seemed to have been a complete collapse of office holders. The Circuit appointed Mr T. Hartley Society Steward, W. Seymour as Musical director and Mr Sheil as Sunday School Superintendent. Three, unnamed, members were appointed to act alongside these three as a management committee. The circuit was still negotiating with the colliery for help with repairs to the building but the membership has collapsed to nine. This reduction had been gradual, but the problems with the Ladies' Bright Hour (not mentioned again) and the questions of impropriety in fund raising must have had an adverse effect on the Society.

Although there was little hint of it in the records of the circuit, this was the start of the Great Depression and young people would be concerned about the state of the economy. William Baugh had passed his written exam for the ministry and things looked positive, but in September it was reported to the local preachers' meeting and the District Committee is informed, that two local preachers had separated from the meeting. William Baugh and John Clarke had gone to Newfoundland as candidates for the Uniting Church ministry. In fact John, of whom we had heard no news regarding his candidature, had arrived in Quebec in July but

William was not to make the journey until September 1932, whether this means that he decided to take up the scholarship at Hartley College before making his move we do not know.

December brought good news for New Sharlston. A letter was received from the Colliery Company offering to do the repairs. The circuit replied with an expression of gratitude and a new committee was appointed, not trustees, as the original committee who were party to agreement with the company had died or had removed. It is to be remembered that this building was the property of the New Sharlston Colliery Company and its use was gifted to the Primitive Methodist Circuit after a vote of those worshipping there. Despite the passage of 61 years there seems still to have been an understanding that the building was owned by the colliery rather than the Society.

The meeting received a letter about Methodist Union and agreed to an exchange of representatives at Quarterly Meetings. They appointed three representatives to attend the Wesleyan meetings and agreed to receive representatives from the Wesleyan Circuit and the United Methodist Circuit and to support united meetings for Methodist Witness. The churches which were related to Normanton were Wakefield Road, St John's and Altofts from the Rothwell Wesleyan Circuit and Hopetown in the Castleford United Methodist Circuit.

In March 1930, a delegation from the Rothwell Wesleyan Circuit, consisting of the Revds T. Morris and F. Rowley and Messrs Nixon, Tattersall and Hailstone were welcomed by the chairman. The meeting, reflecting the situation in Lock Lane, Altofts, recommended that the Trust Boards

Mr. W. Ratcliffe

should carefully consider the need to correct the value of their Trust properties. With the progress at New Sharlston in mind, and the renovations underway, the meeting expressed its thanks to the members from Sharlston Common and Streethouse for their special work in that Society and to Mr and Mrs Bloomfield for permitting services to be held in their house during the renovations. Arrangements were made for a circuit rally at Wakefield Road Primitive Church on May 21st and an invitation to participate was extended to the Wesleyan congregation, the Revd F. Rowley being asked to address the rally.

June brought the news of another early member resigning his post. Mr W. Ratcliffe asked to resign as steward at Lock Lane after 39 years service. It was agreed to accept his resignation and to place his name on the list as honorary steward.

Property values

As was noted earlier Quarterly Meeting had expressed concern that the Trust properties should be revalued for insurance purposes. The following table shows how this was done and includes some information about later changes.

	Built	value 1934
Trinity	1874	£4500
Beckbridge	1903	£1500
Castleford Road	1898	£5000[13]
Altofts (Lock Lane)	1871	£2000

---

[13] In 1945 there is a note that this property was considerably damaged by colliery subsidence. The insurance company have terminated the insurance of this building.

Streethouse	1880	£1850
Sharlston Common	1913	1750
New Sharlston	Rented	NO rent paid
Sunday School	1939	£507[14]
Manse	1897	£750[15]

The New Sharlston schedules are interesting in this respect. As we have seen previously the Church was accepted as the property of the New Sharlston Colliery Company and they had been asked to maintain it, but the schedules show no rent actually paid to the company.

---

[14] After this all income and expenditure is shown in the schedules against the Sunday School and none against the chapel at New Sharlston.
[15] In 1950 the manse in Church Lane is still shown as valued at £750, this would seem completely unrealistic.

CHAPTER FIVE

Towards Union

After several years of discussion and voting in the Wesleyan Methodist Church, the Primitive Methodist Church and the United Methodist Church the three churches agreed in 1929 that they should unite in one body as The Methodist Church. This union was to be enacted in 1932. As will be seen from this account bringing about that unity locally was to be a longer and even more difficult process.

September 1930 brought a new minister to the Primitive Methodist Circuit in Normanton. This was the last Primitive Methodist minister to be appointed to the circuit before Methodist Union. Revd William Jacques and his wife Margaret were to remain in the circuit for the next six years, taking the circuit through the process of union.

His first meeting started with recording the passing of Henry Seymour, 78, who had given 50 years service to Streethouse Church. Henry was a coal miner, as were most of the founders at Streethouse, he and his wife Jane had brought seven children into the world including William who was noted as the Musical Director at New Sharlston, but all seem to have been involved in the church.

Mr Jacques noted that there was no safe in the manse and concern was expressed about the safety of circuit deeds and documents. The stewards were asked to acquire a safe when the opportunity presented itself (i.e. when funds were available).

It was agreed by the meeting that Normanton Circuit of the new Methodist Church would be in the Wakefield and Doncaster District.

The meeting congratulated Sharlston Common Society on the installation of electric light in the church and on meeting the cost.

The finances were discussed and it was agreed that an allocation of 6s per member should be set for the next quarter.

By the middle of 1931 Beckbridge too had installed electric light and had found the £71 cost themselves. Meanwhile Streethouse Church had been redecorated by the voluntary labour of the men of the congregation.

The September Quarterly Meeting saw a series of decisions relating to Union. The meeting received a report of a Connexional appeal to raise £20,000 to make all local preachers eligible for membership of the Wesleyan Local Preachers' Aid Association. A letter from the Leeds District sub-committee followed informing them that Normanton would be expected to raise £35 towards this appeal[16].

It seems that the proposed Wakefield and Doncaster District had been altered to Doncaster and Barnsley District with amended boundaries. The Normanton Circuit sent a request to the appropriate committee to be allowed to remain within the Leeds District. The Boundaries Commission agreed to recommend that Normanton, Wakefield and Castleford remain in the Leeds District.

An exchange of minister for an evening service during the quarter was agreed with Revd Thompson of the Wesleyan Church.

A resolution was brought to the Quarterly Meeting regarding the World Disarmament Conference. It appealed to the governments of the world for a real reduction of the armies, navies and airforces of the world. The formal

[16] Although to our ears £35 does not sound a large sum it is the equivalent of around £1,170 in today's value.

resolution was signed and forwarded through the League of Nations Union.

The Normanton Methodist Council, the body to oversee the local Union arrangements, was set up with members from the Wesleyan Circuit and the Primitive Circuit, no membership is noted from the United Methodists whose only presence at this time is in Hopetown. The first meeting was set for June 8th at Wakefield Road, Wesleyan Church.

In regard to the appeal for £20,000 the Normanton circuit had forwarded £30 to the Local Preachers' Mutual Aid Lightening Fund. It is never clear how such a shortfall would affect the putative membership of the Normanton local preachers.

Discipline for local preachers was still a serious matter and a meeting was convened at Streethouse to examine the case of a local preacher from Sharlston Common who had not fulfilled his obligations, that is, he was failing to attend worship, in particular Holy Communion. The Local Preacher admitted his failings and suggested that he should transfer his membership to Streethouse. This suggestion would indicate some difficulty within the congregation and might be at the root of his failure. The meeting decided to suspend him for six months and then to review his behaviour in regard to fulfilling his obligations. If there was not an improvement his name would be removed from the plan. At the review his name was duly removed.

There had been no mention of a report from the Normanton Methodist Council and the November Quarterly Meeting instructed the secretary to write to the Rothwell Circuit inviting them to consider the regrouping of the churches in the Normanton area. Despite the lack of commitment from Rothwell, Normanton continued to make the changes needed to put the union proposals into effect. The December meeting was arranged to be held at "Trinity" Church, this name change would appear to be a response to the reality of two "Wakefield Road" churches in Normanton.

The Local Preachers' meeting, which had always been a prelude to the Quarterly Meeting was now to be a separate meeting following Wesleyan practice. The meeting resolved to receive the proposed scheme for amalgamation of all the churches in Normanton and Altofts into one circuit and to accept it as a basis for further negotiation.

Amalgamation proposals

In September 1934 a letter of sympathy was sent to the Rothwell Circuit regarding the sudden death of the Revd Allen Holt, Superintendent of the ex-Wesleyan Circuit. This came at a crucial time in the negotiations and may have had some effect on the outcome.

The main business of the meeting was consideration of the proposed scheme for amalgamation:

1.   That the Normanton Circuit be amalgamated with the three Churches - Wakefield Road, Upper Altofts, St John's in the Rothwell ex Wesleyan Circuit with one Quarterly Meeting and one Plan.

2.   That invitations to become part of this Circuit be sent through their respective Quarterly Meetings to Loscoe and Lower Altofts Churches, Castleford ex-W Circuit; and to Hopetown Church Castleford ex U.M. Circuit.

3.   That the Ministerial Staff of the Circuit consist of two approved list ministers.

4.   That the first Superintendent of the Amalgamated Circuit be the Superintendent Minister of the Normanton Circuit at the time of amalgamation.

5.   That No 1 lives at Normanton and No. 2 lives at Altofts.

6.   That Wakefield Road ex-W. Church be regarded as the Head Church of the Circuit.

7.   That the names of the local preachers be placed on the Plan in the order of them coming on Full Plan.

8.   That there be a General Purposes Committee for the Circuit consisting of the Ministers, together with the two Circuit Stewards and one representative from each church.

9.   That the contributions from the various Societies to the Circuit Fund be as listed

10.   That the engagements with the Ministers made by the two Circuits concerned prior to amalgamation be confirmed.

11.   That the Ministers allowances be £270 and £250 a year, with the usual house, postal, and bookroom allowances.

12.   That each Minister be allowed five free Sundays a year including L.P.M.A. Sunday.

13.   That the Scheme be submitted to the next September Quarterly Meeting of each circuit concerned, and if approved, be forwarded through the necessary channels to the 1935 Conference for sanction, so that it may come into operation from the first of September 1935.

This proposal was approved with two suggested amendments to clause 6. "Providing that the superintendent Minister remain in charge of Trinity Church". This was carried unanimously, but was defeated by 30 votes to eight with six neutral by the second amendment "That Trinity Church be regarded as the Head Church of the Circuit.

The next meeting of the circuit received a response from the Rothwell ex-Wesleyan Circuit and a copy of a resolution passed by the Normanton Wakefield Road Methodist Church Leaders' Meeting.

" At the recent Quarterly Meeting of the (Leeds) Rothwell Circuit a long discussion took place on the question of re-arranging the Circuits. It was eventually decided that the present time was very inopportune and that we postpone the question for two years." This letter is signed by W. Ellis, the Quarterly Meeting Secretary.

It was decided to cordially reply to the following resolution passed by the Wakefield Road Wesleyan Church Leaders' Meeting.

" That we as members of the Leaders' Meeting express our deep regret that the Quarterly Meeting of our Circuit decided against the acceptance of the two prepared schemes for a Rothwell and Normanton Circuit under Methodist Union. That we as a meeting and Church pledge ourselves to work for that end which the schemes had in view. Assuring you that at all times we are willing to cooperate in any way by joint meetings or evangelistic work similar to those you have already arranged." This was signed by both the Society Stewards, C. F. Kapper and H. R. Johnson and also by the minister Revd E. Thompson.

This sent everything into limbo.

A long silence

For the next 14 years the Normanton minutes are silent on the matter of amalgamation. As can be deduced from the occasional mention of apparently friendly relations with the Wakefield Road congregation and some mention found in the Rothwell minutes referred to later, there was no actual animosity.

From 1935 the minutes continue to record the life of the ex-Primitive circuit in Normanton. None of the three Castleford churches are mentioned in this respect again.

Membership was recorded at 330 full and 40 on trial and there was some problems with the manse. It was decided to ask the Sanitary Inspector to examine the manse and provide a certificate for the District Chairman. There are no mentions in the minutes of what prompted this action, but as it is during the invitation period for the new minister this may have had some bearing. A Circuit Fete and Sale of Work was organised for the Manse Account which raised £35 11s 6d. This event was held at Hanson House Farm, a substantial property off Snydale Road, which was to be the venue for several circuit events over the next few years.

The Quarterly Meeting drew attention of the schools to the offer of Bibles by the Lord Wharton's Charity. Lord Wharton founded his Bible charity shortly before he died in 1696. He left land near York, which subsequently became known as the Bible Lands, in order to maintain the Trust. This land was sold in 1871, but by then the Trust had built up sufficient financial reserves to maintain its activities right up to the present day.

His intention was to present Bibles to children to be their personal possession (ie not just for use in school or church). Initially Bibles were available in those parts of England where Philip Lord Wharton had lived or owned property, ie Yorkshire, Cumberland, Westmorland and Buckinghamshire, but by the twentieth century this became expanded to include all parts of the United Kingdom. The conditions were that the recipient had to be able to read, and to be able to recite from memory Psalms 1, 15, 25, 37, 101, 113 and 145. Initially 1,050 Bibles were distributed each year; at the time the Normanton Circuit took this up several times that number were being presented. Several local families from Altofts still have one of these bibles in their possession.

A letter is received from the Overseas Mission Fund asking the circuit to raise £10 towards wiping out the debt they have incurred. Sharlston Common, Streethouse, Beckbridge and Castleford Road churches have apparently agreed to raise at least £1 each, the other three churches are to be asked to do what they can and should the whole £10 not be raised in this way, Trinity is to be asked to find the balance.

The question of unaccredited preachers is raised again, this time the problem seems to lie with the invitations of several Baptists to preach in the churches. The Revd Jacques is asked to enquire regarding their status.

With the Wesley Deaconess Convocation due to be held in Leeds in 1936, several requests were received and the circuit wrote to the Order suggesting that Deaconesses could occupy the Castleford Road and New Sharlston pulpits on April 26th and offering financial support if this is needed. In the event, the circuit received the Deaconesses and sent 15s to help pay the expenses of the Convocation.

Ministerial assistance

In December 1935 Mr J. W. Martin presented a resolution to appoint a committee to enquire if it is possible to secure some additional assistance to help the minister with his duties. This was approved by the Quarterly Meeting. The committee was formed and proposals sent out to each of the churches. It seems that about £60 would be needed for a probationer but several of the churches voted against this proposal and the circuit was not been able to go any further. The June 1937 meeting voted in favour of the principle of making application for a probationer for one year provided the contribution from the circuits is not greater than £60. It was decided to send Mr Martin back to those societies who previously voted against, this time accompanied by the minister, to persuade them to vote in favour.

The matter returned to the Circuit twelve months later and a new committee was formed to consider whether satisfactory arrangements could be made for either a probationer or a lay pastor. The committee is to bring their conclusions to the next Quarterly Meeting which would decide whether the matter should go ahead or be withdrawn.

Shortly after this the circuit received a letter from the District to inform them that there was no prospect of their receiving additional ministerial service within the suggested limit of £60 and the June 1938 meeting decided that the matter should not be proceeded with.

The first "Methodist" minister

The Revd Ralph Street succeeded William Jacques in September 1936, the first new minister under the regulations of the new Methodist Church. Mr Street was about 50 years old, an ex-Primitive Methodist minister who came into the circuit with his wife Margaret and her sister Mary Hughes.

One of the first events arranged under the new minister was the "recognition service" of Mr J. Skidmore as a local preacher. In the valedictory service for William Jacques it is mentioned that he had "ordained" several young persons as Local Preachers. This had been the normal usage by the Prims. Although there are occasional slips back to "ordained" in minutes over the following years, the normal understanding moves to a recognition service for local preachers.

The following meeting revisited the matter of unaccredited preachers and rescinded the minute prohibiting the use of preachers not on any recognised plan while recommending that Society stewards be asked to give particular attention to those whom they invite to occupy the pulpit.

Mr John Skidmore was nominated for the ministry and the meeting voted 39 for none against, none neutral. Twelve months later, September 1938 he was accepted for the ministry and went to Wesley Theological College, Headingley Leeds, the first candidate from this circuit not to be sent to Hartley.

A proposed dog racing track at Whitwood was opposed by the circuit and the Quarterly Meeting wrote to the County Council regarding this.

New Sharlston seems to have been reinvigorated and with membership now in the twenties was looking to build a school. In 1938 they received permission to buy land and build a hut. In December 1939 they made application for a loan of £200 from Chapel Aid Association.

The Trustees at Sharlston Common in 1938 are listed as:

Tim Hartley	Colliery deputy
Sarah Ellen Hartley	Married Woman
Annie Briscoe	Widow (Later Mrs Saxton)
Eliza Nightingale	Married Woman
Joseph Nightingale	Insurance agent
Isabella Spires	Married Woman
George Spires	Colliery Deputy
John Richard Green	Byeworker
Rebecca Ward	Married Woman
Emily Wood	Married Woman
George H Bailey	Miner
Eva Bailey	Married woman
Percy Owen	Miner

Ethel Chambers	Spinster (Later as Seymour, Married Woman)
William Ward	Retired
Walter Saxton	Colliery Deputy
Ella Burkinshaw	Married Woman

By 1940 Annie Briscoe was Mrs Saxton and treasurer. She was succeeded in that role in 1942 by Miss Chambers (Ethel Chambers married John Seymour 1948 and died in 1955 at 60 years of age.)

By April 1942 the debt had been reduced to £59 and the treasurer was instructed to pay this off. The money was to come from the Sunday School £12; Ladies Bright Hour, £10; £7 Trust Fund, £7; Peaceful Night Fund, £15; the last £15 being paid by the Chapel Aid Fund.

The war years

The minutes of the September 1939 Quarterly Meeting are brief and largely concerned with finding a minister from 1941. There is no mention of the looming war.

In the March 1940 meeting it was suggested that the Castleford Road Trustees should be asked to approach the Powell Street, Castleford Circuit with the ultimate object of arranging an amalgamation with the Pontefract Road Society. Pontefract Road, was the Hopetown ex-United Methodist Church and despite being on the far fringes of Castleford did not make any move towards Normanton until 1957 by which time Castleford Road itself had been demolished.

At a special meeting to invite a new minister, two names were suggested, Revd L. G. Beardsall of Filey was to be first choice with Revd Charles Wacey of Ashby-de-la Zouch in reserve. A salary of £270 was to be offered with one free Sunday each quarter and two in the holiday quarter. It was also decided that Mr Street should be paid the same for his final year providing that he should agree to the free Sunday arrangement. The number of Sundays were the same, but the disposition was now more rigid and specific and a clear limit on holidays was laid down. In the event Revd Wacey accepted the appointment and was stationed from 1941

It was proposed that the circuit convey to the Connexional authorities the advisability of a general stand still order (of ministers) in view of the war condition. Presumably they intended that this should apply after the new minister arrived.

It was noted in the minutes that The Revd Ralph Street had not missed a single appointment in five years owing to illness. While it is impossible to know how the secretary understood this comment, it does speak volumes about the health of ministers generally.

Throughout the war years the circuit seems to have been well served by the Deaconess caravan missions. Castleford Road church received the services of the connexional caravan for two weeks in January 1942 and, after a request from the circuit, Caravan Hope came to Streethouse, New Sharlston and Sharlston Common in early 1944 with an increase of 14 members resulting.

Designating the Wakefield Mission of 1842 as the start of Primitive Methodism in Normanton, the circuit made plans for centenary celebrations in April 1942. With a birthday party on April 18th, services of celebration attended by past ministers and a souvenir programme for the week which gave a brief outline of the history of the circuit and its churches. The souvenir programme includes a comparison of the membership in 1879 when Normanton became an independent circuit, 193 (with six churches) and a membership in1942 of 356 (seven churches).

Photo on following page:
The Celebration Birthday Party in Trinity Church with Revd Jaques on the left and Revd Wacey on the right. Mrs Jane Seymour, the oldest connecting member, is cutting the cake.

Mr Skidmore has successfully completed his training and after four years at Headingley he is taking up a circuit appointment.

At the June 1942 Quarterly the secretary drew attention to the fact that Streethouse, New Sharlston and Sharlston Common were not connected with Normanton Council of Christian Congregations. It was proposed that they should be brought into membership as soon as possible.

The New Sharlston Society, which had taken on the building of the Sunday School in September 1939 at a cost of £500 were able to report in March 1943 that the debt had been cleared. Even without the difficulties the Society had been through, this would have been a considerable achievement.

At the end of year Quarterly, the circuit received a report about the meagre attendance of both scholars and staff at the Castleford Road Sunday School and arranged for a deputation to find an answer to this situation. Although nothing further is reported on this matter, within a year Castleford Road had only one Trustee. This was because the building was so badly damaged by subsidence that it was dangerous. It seems that many of the members had decided that safety came first and there followed an exodus to Beckbridge. In March 1945 the circuit recommended that worship in the premises should be discontinued owing to the unsafe state of the building. It was suggested that the organ should be sold as it was at risk. Any funds raised should be used for the purposes of the Castleford Road Methodist Church. The one remaining Trustee, Mr Baines, pleaded for a reduction in the allocation because of the transfer of members but clearly worship was continuing in the premises and in September 1945 the circuit accepted Mr Baines's offer of two thirds of the allocation and appointed new Trustees. All efforts to gain compensation from the Coal Board were unsuccessful as the mine had been closed prior to Nationalisation. The structure was crumbling and this would seem to have been a misplaced loyalty.

During all of the war period there were only two mentions in the Quarterly Minutes of that event, the first regarding stationing and in 1944 a complaint about inadequate coke supplies. It is difficult to imagine how nothing worth recording about the war impinged on the life of the circuit.

Revd Wacey had been re-invited for 1944-45 by a unanimous vote and for the following year by a vote of 29 for with four neutral and there was no invitation to remain after that time. In the vote of thanks to Charles Wacey recorded in the minutes his wife is mentioned for her good work especially with young people and, unusually, their servant Josephine Tonks is given thanks for the work she had done in the church. This same meeting spent some time discussing the manse and decided that it was unsuitable for its purpose and that a new premises should be bought as early as possible. Despite this, No 39 Church Lane remained in use until 1968 when both it and Patience Lane were disposed of to buy a manse at Field End, Station Road.

The Revd B. Tinkler had accepted an invitation for 1946-47 but, after consideration, withdrew his offer. The committee agreed that there should be no further invitations until after Conference and in December the Invitation Committee met with Revd William Russell Hall and his wife Ruth. They agreed to accept an invitation, the meeting affirming this by vote.

CHAPTER SIX

The Wesleyan Story

There was never a Normanton Wesleyan Methodist Circuit. But the Wesleyans had a considerable presence in the area from early on, first as part of the Wakefield Wesleyan Methodist Circuit and then in the shape of Rothwell Wesleyan Circuit, an offshoot of Wakefield.

The Wakefield Wesleyan Methodist Circuit has a very long history. It was established in 1787 and grew steadily over the next hundred years from an initial membership of 670 served by two ministers to a membership of 1546 served by four ministers. This large and geographically dispersed circuit had 19 churches in 1892. It was in this year that the division took place which eventually led to a union with the Normanton church.

Wakefield's Normanton fringe

The earliest of the Wesleyan churches in the Normanton area was actually in the village of Altofts. Its history was quite difficult to trace as there are a variety of dates given for the building. Some church publications date it from 1833, but give no provenance for this date. There is an article from the Normanton and District Advertiser of 1st March 1929 which gives a date of 1838. Part of the difficulty has, no doubt, been the loss of Church Minute Books in the fire of 1886 which gutted the building. Fortunately one record book seems to have survived. The Church Accounts for 1842-1877 was not part of this destruction and has made its way to the Wakefield Archives. What the accounts show is the detailed cost of buying the land and constructing the church which commenced in 1842 and was completed in time for an opening in July 1843.

The society in Altofts had first appeared on the Wakefield plan in 1809 and continued to be shown until 1820 when it disappeared. It reappears as a preaching place in 1824 for a few years but does not become a permanent presence until 1838. The society met in a variety of buildings during this time and, although there are competing claims in the various brief circuit histories produced for anniversaries, it seems likely that it was the Wesleyans who met in the buildings at Greystones.

Most startling are the membership figures which appear in the Wakefield minutes of the period. In 1850 Altofts has a recorded membership of 3 which only grows to 15 in 1855. From this point onwards the growth is steady if not spectacular, climbing steadily to 46 members in 1885. Although this might seem surprising for a new church, the fluctuating fortunes of the previous decades suggest that this may not be too unusual. There are also figures given for some of the churches in the area which offer very small membership but attendance many times larger.

To the south of Normanton, Wakefield had a further outpost in Sharlston. The brief history of this society shows a degree of cooperation between the Primitive Methodist Circuit and the Wesleyans. In 1850 Sharlston appears on the Wakefield plan with 13 members, rising spectacularly to 50 members in 1855. This growth was not maintained and the numbers started to fall again. In 1868 the Crossleys, who owned the mine built a new church and there was a ballot amongst all the chapel people in the village as to who would have responsibility for it. The ballot went to the Prims and the Wesleyan circuit removed Sharlston from its plan.

In Normanton, the Wesleyans first met in a disused library room on the railway station, the first service being held on April 13th 1862, conducted by a local preacher, Mr T. O. Quibell. In 1867 Wakefield agreed to buy a site for the building of a church and school in Normanton. In the following March the project was begun on the site in Wakefield Road. The membership at Normanton was given as ten when it appeared in the accounts for the first time.

Whilst the membership at Altofts continued to fluctuate, the Normanton society built steadily to a peak of 124 in 1885, this strength perhaps contributing to the drive for separation.

The New Circuit

In March 1892, the Leeds Rothwell Circuit started its new independent life with a membership of 494 and 35 on trial members. Alongside these there were 90 young people enrolled in the juvenile classes. The two principal societies were Rothwell and Normanton and it would seem that, throughout the life of this circuit, there was a tension between the needs of these two and something of a struggle to support the six smaller societies.

The superintendent was to be the Revd William Stewart, who had already served the Wakefield Circuit for two years and would continue to live at Rothwell in the minister's house. A new minister, Reverend Herbert Nicholls was appointed to live at Normanton where the circuit was committed to buying a new house. The minister's house at Normanton was estimated to cost £500 and was to be paid for at £25 per quarter over four years, a major commitment for a new circuit. The practice in such circumstances was to ask the District to appoint a "young man", that is an unmarried minister, to the circuit until a house was acquired. In such an arrangement the minister would be found lodgings in the area in which he was to serve, which may have contributed to the difficulties in keeping a minister in the Normanton section over the next few years. After less than a year in post, Herbert Nicholls told the circuit that he would be leaving at the next Conference and, despite efforts to dissuade him, he left in September 1893. William Stewart was also leaving at this time, but this was an expected change as he had been at Rothwell for three years.

The new staff, the Revd E Workman as Superintendent at Rothwell and the Revd E Coulson to be the minister at Normanton came into a circuit in which there were already problems, which were exacerbated by Mr Coulson leaving almost immediately. At the time, the minutes suggest that the circuit did not know where he had gone and that it seemed he had left the ministry.[17] After about four weeks another young minister, the Revd Ebenezer Bulmer, was sent from the President's Reserve to fill the vacancy.

At this early point in the circuit's life, financial troubles were to add to the stresses. The Rothwell house had been in need of repair and renovation when the new minister came and the cost was stated to be £90. The Quarter's payment towards the new manse at Normanton was not paid. It was decided that the payments should be suspended for two further quarters, owing, it was said, to the depressed condition of trade. This was also the time of the mine unrest with strikes taking place throughout Yorkshire. The society at Normanton, which was also struggling to make their quarterly payments, felt this was a breaking of faith and the treasurer, Mr McAdoo protested to the meeting.

The March 1894 Quarterly Meeting passed the accounts including the cost of repairs to the Rothwell manse, totalling £86 15s 6d. This left the circuit indebted to the stewards for £69 14s 11d.[18] In principle, Methodists would not incur a debt outside the society, debtors had to be paid. This principle put a heavy load on those willing to act as stewards

---

[17] A note in the 1947 Souvenir Booklet produced by the circuit claims that he was later the District Secretary.
[18] This would be the equivalent of a debt of £4,200 in today's terms.

and the circuit struggled to repay these "loans" for a considerable time.

The June meeting brought little change. The meeting was told that the expectations that Wakefield Circuit had, at the point of division, not been met and it was unreasonable to expect the stewards to continue to meet the £25 levy towards the Normanton house from their own pockets. By September, this debt had been reduced to £23 3s 2d with the aid of a special tea. These special efforts continued and it was reported to the December meeting that the debts on the Superintendent's house had been cleared. The payments to the reserve fund were to be continued.

Both Mr Bulmer and Mr Workman had been re-invited for a further year and this was to be repeated in the spring to give them three years in the circuit.

The spring meeting in 1895 showed a fluctuating membership with 478 plus 74 on trial. The year had brought 31 removals, 13 deaths and 72 received into membership. This wide movement seems to have been fairly usual for the time which may have been influenced by the changing employment situations in some of the society areas.

Although there was now a surplus in the General Account of £7 12s 4d this was not a comfortable cushion and only £17 was paid into the reserves (the house fund).

A committee meeting in July considered the financial situation, particularly in the light of the plan to move to two married ministers and a new house. The reserve fund stood at £160 and the Normanton people were asked to start looking for suitable houses or sites and to report back. This positive move was followed by the purchase of a desk for the Normanton minister for immediate use, but to be considered as part of the furnishings of the new house. The house committee met again in December to consider one or two likely sites and to agree the salary of the second minister, which was set at £150 per annum. The Quarterly Meeting, attended by both ministers, two stewards and 40 members was a social affair. The minutes describe it: "Previous to the business meeting, the members sat down to dinner together, which had not only been beautifully prepared and tastefully laid by the ladies of the Normanton Society, but the gentlemen were most assiduously waited upon by them, and their every want promptly and pleasantly supplied."

In the business meeting the sites for the Normanton House were discussed. It was proposed that Sir Matthew Dodsworth be approached about a site in Wesley Terrace, Altofts and the best possible terms arranged. A building committee was formed and, after some discussion, a Mr Thornton of Wakefield was proposed as the architect to approach. It was felt that the total cost should not exceed £600, including land, conveyancing and plans. The cost of the land was to be paid out of the funds now in the bank.

The financial discussion reveals both optimism and reality. The expenditure with two men (sic) would amount to £469 though the present income was only £385. The circuit had been raising about £30 a year in special efforts and had a ten year diminishing grant of £40 per annum. Clearly, even with the full value of the grant, this would not cover the anticipated outgoings.

Despite the straitened circumstances of the circuit, Carlton was given permission to rebuild the church. This dichotomy of commitment to local and circuit situations appears in the minutes regularly.

Not all of the Circuit Meeting's interest is focussed on finance. A memorial from this meeting was sent to Her Majesty's Government "For the duty of at once taking active measures for putting a stop to the inhuman and tyrannical treatment by the Sultan of Turkey of his Christian subjects in Armenia in fulfilment of pledges entered into at the Berlin Conference." Despite its size and situation, the circuit was attempting to operate on an international stage.

A New House

It seems that the earlier negotiations had not been fruitful and, in March 1896, a piece of land was purchased on the Altofts Road with plans for a "four square house" prepared. The tenders for the building had been received and it was agreed to accept the tender of a Mr Bramhall for all trades other than joinery which was to be provided by Mr Denniston. The agreed costs were to be £479 for Mr Bramhall, £131 to Mr Denniston, Land £90 and architects fees of £30. After paying for the land and the expenses of about £85 there was £140 remaining in the reserve fund for the furnishings.

The June meeting included notes of thanks for both Mr Bulmer, who was leaving at the end of the term, and Mr Workman, who was also leaving the superintendent's post to be replaced by Revd J. B. Maltby. Included in the thanks for Mr Workman were regrets for the "unfortunate circumstances under which he came", and the trouble at Normanton. No further clarification of these problems is given, although the sudden departure of Mr Coulson must have featured in the Normanton problem. A lengthy statement of gratitude for the work of Miss Workman was also given to the meeting, along with personal testimonies to her character. She had been involved in circuit life, not only as pianist, organist and a mission leader, but had had considerable influence on young men and women in the circuit, both as a speaker and a confidant.

The Temperance Society reported 717 persons in the Band of Hope and 218 adult members in the circuit. Since there were 525 adult members in the circuit these numbers suggest a less enthusiastic commitment than suggested by the children's membership.

The Normanton house was on target to be ready for the new minister and it was agreed to colour wash the walls. Mr

Workman was requested to negotiate a further loan of £300 which was expected to involve 3½% interest. In the event Mr Denton, the treasurer was able to report to the September meeting that the loan had been procured and that the house would be ready for furnishing within a week. It was decided to grant the Normanton stewards £10 per quarter to meet the expenses of the house, such as rates and maintenance. The first occupants of the new manse in Patience Lane were Revd John Tyreman and his wife Sarah, a young couple from North Yorkshire, recently married. The Superintendent minister, stationed at Rothwell, was Rev J. Brampton Maltby. These two minsters were to serve the circuit for three years through some difficult financial struggles.

The meeting also discussed the coming Conference to be held in Leeds in 1897. It was agreed that the superintendent and stewards would form a committee to to deal with any arrangements for the circuit's involvement in this. Armenia had not been forgotten, the meeting passing a further motion concerning the "fiendish atrocities" being perpetrated on the Armenian Christians by the army of Turkey.

The last meeting in 1896 received membership figures of 525 with 29 on trial. Revd Maltby was invited for a further year and accepted. For the first time, the minutes record the stewards' intention to attend Synod and to appoint another representative. Perhaps this was a sign of maturing within the circuit which was, after all, still very young. The final cost of the Normanton Manse as completed was £721 1s 6d and the furnishings had cost £206 4s 2d. This was funded by a combination of the reserve fund and a loan for the bulk of the house building cost. The circuit were, in theory, committed to putting aside £25 per quarter to pay this loan, but this was to be the subject of an ongoing struggle. Despite this reality, a scheme for the enlargement of the school at Normanton Wesleyan at a cost of £500 was presented and agreed. This differentiation between the funding of local church projects and the costs of the circuit crop up at intervals throughout the years.

A more full account of the membership of the circuit was given to the Quarterly Meeting in June 1897 with a slight increase in the adult membership to 531 with 48 on trial. There were, however, 1279 Sunday School scholars, served by 194 teachers. To a great extent this large membership of the Sunday School is at the root of the memories of packed churches, especially on Anniversary Sundays.

The following two years were stable with few changes or troubles. The most notable event was the permission given by the circuit for the building of the proposed mission church at St John's in Normanton. It was made clear that the responsibility for this new project was to be borne by the Normanton Society, the Normanton people taking on the financial and administrative responsibility for the St John's Terrace mission without any question. It was only the staffing which was to cause a degree of friction in the years to come.

March 1899 foreshadowed a change in the circuit staffing with the two incumbents preparing to move on at the next Conference. Invitations were offered to the Revd Arnold to be the next superintendent and Revd William Salisbury to be the minister at Normanton.

Despite what appears to have been a stable period in the circuit's life, the debt on the Normanton Manse still caused concern and a decision was taken to try to decrease the debt by £100 by May. After some discussion, it was decided that the £40 a year allowed to the circuit stewards should be allotted to the Normanton House.

The section of the circuit which is our particular concern returned membership figures of 157 at Normanton and 21 at Altofts. Attendance records suggest that there were many more people involved at Altofts than on the membership or it would have been difficult to explain the continuing work on buildings etc.

Finances continued to be a cause for concern for the circuit the deficit having grown from £29 3s 3d to £32 13s 5d. A member of the meeting asked whether it was advisable to have an offertory at every service, a question which seems astonishing today.

The Normanton house was still a cause for concern and although the stewards had £30 in hand there was £76 10s further needed to meet the conditions of the loan. Mr Seanor offered to provide £20 if the whole sum could be raised immediately and Mr McAdoo pledged £25 from Normanton. The meeting anticipated gifts from several people not present at the meeting in the hope that the total sum would be found.

Twentieth Century

The New year and new century started with the Wesleyans of Normanton and Altofts still in some uncertainty. The St John's Terrace project seems to have been well established in that the circuit had now allocated a quarterly contribution directly to that Society. The three societies in what was to be the Normanton circuit were asked for: Normanton £30, Altofts £3 10s and St John's Terrace £1. The circuit nominated two candidates for the ministry, one of whom was Mr Barton Wesley McAdoo from Normanton who was received into the ministry in 1903 and died in 1951. The schedules at the time list the values of the churches: Altofts was given as £600 and Normanton as £2,500. Clearly with the school premises, this was a substantial property. No value was shown for St John's Terrace, but as we have seen, it was the responsibility of the Normanton Society and would be listed in their assets, if at all.

The unrest that still seemed to simmer in the circuit came to the surface at the September meeting when a Mr Righton of Normanton gave notice that he wished to bring a resolution to the next meeting to return Normanton and St John's to the Wakefield circuit, offering "its unnatural geographical boundary and the spiritual depression which exists" as his reasons for this move. The resolution was indeed brought to the March meeting, but now he had included the Altofts and Stanley churches. In discussion it appeared that Mr Righton had not consulted Altofts or Stanley and, in fact, Wakefield had not been asked for their view. The matter was concluded at the March meeting when Mr Righton withdrew his resolution as he had discovered that Wakefield did not wish to have Normanton! That the original division of the Wakefield circuit had come about because of disaffection at Normanton may have had some bearing on the response.

Meanwhile Normanton asked for permission to buy a new organ at the cost £450. The society was quite strong with more than 150 members and, despite the apparent unrest, the work seemed to have been going well.

Mr Salisbury was preparing to move on, but he and his wife Martha were also celebrating the arrival of their second son. The circuit was preparing to invite Revd Robert Whitehead as replacement for Mr Salisbury. Robert was a minister of much the same background as William Salisbury. The son of a farmer from Pateley Bridge, he was married with two very young children. The house in Patience Lane was proving its worth, if still not paid for.

1902 brought little ease for the circuit or Normanton. The May meeting agreed that each church in the circuit, except Ouzlewell, should give up one Sunday evening service a Quarter in succession so that St John's Terrace could have one ministerial service a quarter. This harks back to Normanton's original complaint of shortage of ministerial services. June brought a reminder of financial difficulties with a resolution calling on all members to attend class more often and reminding them that they should each contribute one penny a week and one shilling a quarter.

These financial straits brought about an acrimonious discussion at circuit about the relative giving of Normanton and Rothwell. This brought to the fore the reality that the problem lay, not with either church, who were each meeting their agreed commitments, but with the smaller churches, in particular Stanley, which had suffered a severely diminished income. Nevertheless, this again demonstrated a lack of cohesion between the two major churches in the circuit and their satellites.

By December 1902 the Normanton section of the Leeds Rothwell Circuit was showing signs of struggle. The membership of its churches had changed over the previous ten years for the worse:

	1893	1902
Normanton	140	101
Altofts	21	17
St John's	0	15[19]

Despite these diminishing numbers and struggles to meet the needs of the wider circuit, both Normanton and Altofts had found monies for improvements within their own premises.

Financial troubles and continuing disagreements

A positive note was struck in February 1904 with the invitation of the Deaconess Evangelist Jeannie Banks to visit the circuit. She had first visited at the end of a mission in Pontefract Circuit and had then agreed to this appointment. The Deaconess Evangelists (there were two at this time) were much sought after and their appointments throughout the connexional year were made under the auspices of the

---

[19] St Johns appears to show growth, but it was a new start in 1893 and this is slow progress for ten years of effort

Wesley Deaconess Order. Sister Jeannie's mission was reported as producing a large number of enquiries.

Sadly, by the end of the year, further difficulties came to a head. The December Quarterly Meeting received a proposal from Normanton:

"That we make a special grant of £2 10s 0d to the next Quarterly Board and that our future quarterly contributions be £20 providing:

1.   That we have six ministerial appointments per quarter
2.   That the Normanton minister be relieved of the oversight of Oulton, to come into force at the next change of Minister.
3.   That Rothwell make a similar promise to keep up its £40 contribution.
4.   That a small committee be appointed to investigate the financial condition of the circuit and report to the next Quarterly Meeting."

In response to these proposals two resolutions were proposed:

1.   That Normanton be asked to raise its contributions to £30 unconditionally as Rothwell has done.

This was lost by 5 votes for and 7 against.

2.   That a committee be formed to examine thoroughly into the financial and other questions relating to the circuit.

This was carried.

The Circuit Finance Committee, at its meeting on March 3rd 1905, was presented with statistics for the income and outgoings of the circuit over the past years, culminating in the fact that the circuit had been running a quarterly deficit of between £40 and £50. A proposal was put to the meeting that they consider a scale of income from each church on a similar basis to that proposed in 1900. Rothwell and other churches in the circuit agreed to try to raise their proportions but the representatives from Normanton declined to agree the proportion set for them.

The meeting reconvened on March 16th after Normanton had held a Leaders' Meeting at which the following resolution had been passed: "That we cannot see our way clear to contribute more than £27 10s a quarter until such time as our resolution of December 22 1904 be considered in its entirety." My sense is that each of the churches would struggle to meet the new assessments but it is the fact that Normanton was not saying that it could not pay, but was laying a condition on the payment which caused the greatest upset.

The secretary's response reveals the underlying tensions between the two largest churches. He bluntly drew attention to the fact that in his words "Normanton was the cause of the division of the circuit from Wakefield and that Rothwell was better off in every way previous to the division."

In an attempt to resolve the dispute, it was suggested that some of the ministerial services at some of the smaller churches be diminished and added to the provision for Normanton. The committee urged Normanton Leaders' Meeting to reconsider raising their contribution.

The deficit continued to rise and, by the May Finance Committee, had reached £80. The meeting heard a proposal for a circuit effort but it was decided this was not feasible as "Rothwell and Normanton were too far apart". Instead a straightforward allocation of a proportion of this debt was made to each church. This was set at Rothwell £30, Normanton £20, Carlton £5, Stanley £5, Woodlesford £5, Altofts £5, Ouzlewell Green £2 10s, Oulton £5, St John's £2 10s. It is notable that St John's was given its own allocation.

By the June circuit meeting it could be reported that most of the requirements set by Normanton had been met and the society had agreed to raise its contribution to £30. The other decisions of the finance committee in regard to the debt were agreed and it was suggested that they should try to raise these monies by the Christmas meeting. The stewards were also able to report a further increase in membership since the last quarter bringing the total membership up to 579. Despite the settlement, the unrest at Normanton was again evidenced in a proposal to move the manse from Altofts to Normanton.

The house committee met at the manse in Patience Lane, Altofts in September, where the new minister, Revd Herbert William Pates, showed them around. The committee agreed that the manse was in good order but the matter of its distance from Normanton proper should be considered. It was decided to recommend that the circuit should look for a suitable house in the centre of Normanton.

Christmas came and went but the debt was not cleared. Despite the disagreements throughout the past year Normanton, Altofts and St John's, along with Rothwell provided the contributions allocated to them. By the March Circuit Meeting, Carlton and Stanley had made the full contribution, Woodlesford and Oulton had found a part but Ouzlewell Green had not managed anything. The deficiency at the end of this Quarter was £47 6s 11d which meant that the income was still not covering their outgoings. They had managed to raise all but about £5 of the debt from the previous year but had accumulated more than £40 of new debts. The new circuit steward, Mr Stephenson, told the meeting that he and his colleague, Mr Denton, had made up their minds to start their new period of office by clearing the debt. Mr Denton was seriously ill at the time, but they had raised £60 which cleared the debt leaving them £12 13s 1d in hand.

The following year was one of apparent calm with a good financial report having, for the first time since the circuit was formed, ended with a credit balance. The manses were in good repair and the circuit had been happy to approve Mr G. B. Savage, a candidate for the ministry. The membership was down, although the meeting was told that this was contributed to by 13 who should have been removed long ago.

The situation for the ministers had not been so fortunate. For a large part of the time the Revd Herbert Pates had been ill and unable to fulfil his ministry. Some time after his return to work James Duff, the Superintendent had a serious breakdown and, during most of 1907, his duties were undertaken by Revd Herbert Benn, who had also been the supply during Mr Pates illness. No details of the ill health which had caused this long period of absence for Mr Pates, and seemingly other members of his family, are given but he seems to have made a good recovery and is last recorded as superintendent in the Tunstall Circuit 25 years later. Revd Duff was not to recover and the synod made the maximum grant to him as well as the maximum payment for removal of a supernumerary. This last may have been necessary as he was retiring, at only 62, back to County Down in his native Ireland.

The proposal to move the manse from Patience Lane to Normanton was withdrawn towards the end of 1907 owing, it seems, to the large cost of renovation and refurnishing of the manse at Rothwell. The stewards had to spend £50[20] on this work.

The connexional evangelist, Revd E. Davidson, conducted a week's mission at Rothwell in November, a fairly regular feature of the year, though Normanton and Altofts did not appear to be included in these visits nor to invite the evangelist themselves.

A memorial to Conference was moved by the Circuit Steward, Mr Stephenson. This stated "That it was desirable that steps should be taken to amalgamate the theological colleges from four to one." Clearly this did not receive support at Conference!

---

[20] About £2,800 in today's value.

The memorial did not receive overwhelming support at the Circuit Meeting in June, receiving 7 votes for, 4 against and 14 neutral. This meeting was the first of a series of summer meetings which were held at the home of a Mr and Mrs Cook of the Grange, Woodlesford, who provided a generous meal beforehand served, weather permitting, on the lawn.

Both the Superintendent and Revd Pates had moved on that year. The new Normanton minister was Revd Arnold Crawshaw and the Circuit welcomed both Mr Crashaw and his family and Revd Sunderland his father-in-law who came as a supernumerary which seems to have been a temporary arrangement as Revd Sunderland did not remain in the circuit, he and his wife settling elsewhere.

The arrival of new ministers had brought about the painting and refurnishing of the ministers' houses which caused an increase in the deficiency from £41 to £73. Efforts were immediately put in hand to raise the funds to reduce the deficit and the December meeting was pleased to hear that the accounts were back in balance, with the debt cleared.

Although 1909 opened with a valuation of all property, churches, manses and schools of £15,450 without financial problems other than the continuing debt on the Altofts manse which remained at £500, reducing membership raised concerns. These were to continue right through 1910 and on into 1912 sliding year on year down to a low of 445. The summer meeting was moved to Carlton House, the home of County Councillor Mr Hargreaves, the senior circuit steward, who was also generous in helping to clear that year's deficit. The meeting was held in Mr Hargreaves' sitting room and was attended by 45 people

The Conference of 1910 carried a motion that women should be eligible as members of Conference. At this time there were no women in any circuit office in the local circuit.

The circuit treasurer, Mr Stephenson, continued to be concerned that the debt on the Altofts manse remained unpaid. He pointed out that the interest had amounted to £186 in the eleven years since the manse had been acquired and proposed that the loan should be paid off by 1912, which would be the twentieth anniversary of the circuit. Mr Stephenson was appointed to lead the effort and over the next year he was able to raise £35 with a further £42 promised. Normanton received a new minister in 1911. The Revd Maddison Phillipson B.A., a widower of 41,had lost his young wife five years earlier.

The membership had risen to 445 by the end of the year but there were still financial problems and the general accounts show that each of six circuit officers made personal contributions of one guinea to the circuit funds.

The Leaders' Meeting in Normanton at the beginning of 1913 lists the following members: Messrs Appleby, Armitage, Sefton, Marsden, Beilby, J. W. Blackburn, Mrs Armitage, Mrs Arthur Denton, Mrs Beilby and Mrs Nixon. Despite these numbers, Revd Phillipson had to tell the meeting that he had been unable to find anyone who would consent to be nominated as Society Stewards. His solution to this difficulty was to nominate Messrs Appleby and Blackburn whom the meeting appointed. Mr G. W. Denton, a draper from High Street, Normanton, was appointed choirmaster.

The manse fund now stood at £90 9s 6d although there were promises of a further £132 4s.

The Normanton Leaders spent much of 1913 discussing the purchase of individual communion cups, presumably having used a common cup prior to this time. After the matter had been raised at several meetings it was proposed by Mrs Appleby in November that they should buy the best set of cups offered and that £3 18s 6d had been raised for this purpose. The circuit still had a debt to clear and Normanton had been allocated £20 of that needed to clear it. Mr Phillipson was asked to confer with Mr Denton as to how to raise it.

It seems that St Johns was still struggling and that this now involved the provision of leaders from within the congregation. St Johns was never constituted as a Society, being a daughter church of Normanton. The minister was asked to approach Messrs Gallilli, Taylor, Chandler, Sadler, C. H. Blackburn, Gooder and Wood to see if they would give assistance. The Prims had used a similar seeding process to reinvigorate Beckbridge.

First World War and Beyond

Upper Altofts had started looking into acquiring land for a new Sunday School at the beginning of 1913, negotiations having started with Sir Matthew Dodsworth. A number of schemes were being looked at.

Towards the end of 1914 a regular request came before the Normanton Leaders' Meeting, a retiring collection outside the church gates by the Salvation Army. This was granted as was generally the case.

The new minister in Normanton and Altofts, Revd J. Wilson[21] came into the circuit as the First World War began. He was to remain until the close of hostilities. The Society Stewards appointed at the September meeting were Mr Gooder and Mr Harris.

Mrs Nixon, who was a stalwart of the women's work in Normanton, having been President of the sewing group and now responsible for the Sisterhood, reported in 1915 that they now had 98 members and an average attendance of 70. The Sisterhood had just introduced a magazine which was

---

[21] As the Circuit minutes for this period are missing there are few sources for identifying the ministers of this period. It seems likely that this would have been the Revd John Wilson who entered the ministry in 1904 and died in 1954. In 1911 he was a 31 year old probationer in Blackpool and seems to have been accompanied by his older sister.

to be successful. Certainly continuing throughout the war years. The sewing meeting was a redoubtable force, their fundraising a great source of income for Normanton church.

One of the regular occurrences in church minutes at the time of a change of minister was a check on membership and this time the number of members who did not pay their class money was raised. It was decided that there should be a meeting of class leaders to decide the proper roll and to encourage the Class Leaders to persuade the doubtful members to attend class again. Assessment was based on membership which was related to the class rolls. The class monies were of considerable importance to the budget for a church.

A recurring problem in Altofts was that of land and building. In 1914 there was a problem of damage done to the church building owing to subsidence. In April the Society Stewards, Messrs Garrat and Bramham and Mr Stone, the treasurer, met with a Mr Clegg who was representing Pope and Pearson's mine regarding this problem. Mr Clegg agreed that the problem was indeed one of subsidence and agreed that the steps and wall should be repaired as soon as possible, all of which would suggest that there was an active colliery gallery beneath the church. Some arrangement with the company may have been in place as the 1915 Trustees Meeting has an entry expressing thanks for their annual subscription. Individual communion glasses were discussed, two years after the Wakefield Road Society had taken this step, and the Trustees agreed to their purchase if the funds could be raised.

The meeting had also made reference to the shortage of Trustees owing to death and retirement. A special meeting was convened to appoint a new body.
Appointed were:
William Stephenson, Rothwell, Secretary to a Limited Company

Arthur William Seanor, Rothwell, Manager of a firelighter
    Company
John Richard Rogers, Altofts, Railway Signalman
Thomas Arthur Stone, Altofts, Clerk
Herbert Newsome, Altofts, Shop Assistant
Tom Zaccheus Steel, Altofts, Council Road Foreman
Mark Beevers, Altofts, Colliery Banksman
Thomas Marshal, Altofts, Coal Miner
John Mark Stone, Altofts, Clerk
Arthur Harris, Altofts, Draper
Charles Stringer, Altofts, Railway Signalman
Ernest George Smith, Altofts, Clerk

It is noticeable that, although Church Leaders' Meetings
were chaired by the local minister, Trustees Meetings were
chaired by the Superintendent, at this time Revd Nicholas
W. Thomlinson.

Although there were few references to the war in any of
the minute books I have consulted, the November 1917
Normanton Leaders' meeting contains a proposal to send
letters to Mr John and Mrs Sarah Nixon of The Poplars,
Church Lane, Normanton on the loss of their son John
Herbert Nixon, a 20 year old private in the Prince of Wales
Own Civil Service Rifles who died fighting the Turks in what
is now Israel. Arthur Langley, the son of Samuel and Emma
Langley of Market Street Normanton, was 35 years old when
he was killed while serving with the West Yorkshire
Regiment at the Battle of Ypres.

In Upper Altofts there are no direct references. This may
be because of the absence of Leaders' Minutes, but in 1921
the Trustees did authorise a memorial to be erected in the
church. This marble plaque is still to be seen at the back of
the worship area in the new church.

The interior renovation of Upper Altofts was carried out in
1917 at a total cost of £30, including new linoleum for the
aisles and the body of the church and carpet for the pulpit

and around the communion area. The caretaker was to be paid £9 per year for all the work in the church.

As the time approached for invitations to a new minister, plans were made for a welcome tea and two ladies offered to "beg" for the tea. This usage may seem somewhat archaic, but it does clearly describe what was being undertaken.

In August, just before the change of minister, it was decided that St Johns and Wakefield Road should be amalgamated. There were to be an extra Society Steward and Poor Steward appointed to be responsible for St Johns. The new minister, William John Page, son of a serving minister, was an almost exact contemporary of John Wilson, having entered the ministry in 1906 at the age of 25 and dying in 1954.

An invitation was extended to the National Children's Home Choir, who were travelling in the area, to give a concert on Thursday September 30, the money raised would be for NCH.

Mr Blackburn and Mr Gooder proposed the implementation of an envelope scheme. This was the first time such a venture had been suggested. The proposal was agreed. It is likely that Wakefield Road Wesleyan church was the first in the area to implement it.

At Altofts, pew rents had always been a source of finance but in November 1918 it was proposed that they should be abolished. Mr Rogers and Mr Stringer proposed that a letter be sent to all seat holders asking them if they agreed to this or to express their views. At the same time they were asked if they would subscribe annually to the fund in lieu of rent. At the annual meeting it was reported that 14 were in favour and had promised giving amounting to £7 5s 0d, 3 were against and a further 14 were neutral. Since the amount raised by seat rents was £2 12s 6d, it was agreed to abolish pew rents and the system of free seating be inaugurated. Since the meeting also proposed that the seats at present in the possession of seat holders be honoured, one can see how this would create problems for years to come.

The other problem which came into being around this time was the purchase of land for an extension. This land was bought from the Local Government Board at a cost of 2s per yard and the solicitor consulted was Sir William Middlebrook of Leeds. In March a letter was received from Sir William in reference of the Board's legal right to sell the land and recommending that the Trustees proceed with the purchase. This was not the end of the story as in 1921, Mr Stephenson was again asked to act as a deputation to Sir Matthew Dodsworth in regard to an amiable understanding of the boundaries and conveniences of the land. This was despite Revd A. J. Bromwich having a copy of the deeds showing the boundary belonging to the trustees right up to the wall of the adjoining house. There was a clothes post on the land which had been in use by the adjoining cottagers for some time and in 1922 the tenants of the cottages agreed to pay 1s each new year for use of the ground for the clothes post. This was probably to make clear ownership by the church and permission granted.

The new Society Stewards at Normanton appointed in January 1921 were both butchers, Charles Frederick Kappes, of German descent, and Herbert Cressey, both living and trading in Normanton.

Two members, unnamed, proposed that only those interested in the church should receive support from the Poor Fund. No decision on this is recorded, but there does not seem to have been any change in the process of distributing the Poor fund.

The perennial question of the welcome of strangers was raised at the May meeting. The result was the decision "that the members of the Leaders Meeting do this (sic) best to welcome all strangers to our services."

Mr Frederick Nott, who was the Society Steward for St Johns and a member of the Leaders Meeting at Wakefield

Road reported that "we are not getting our fair share of ministerial appointments". It may be remembered that this was the original complaint which led to the break with Wakefield Wesleyan Circuit and which had been repeated within the Rothwell Circuit in the past.

Although there has been no record of its ceasing, a discussion took place in June 1922 about the collection for the poor at sacramental services and a decision was taken to resume the practice. There were regular calls on the fund and Revd Page brought such a matter to the notice of the meeting. He had, he said, engaged a taxi at a cost of 15s to remove a poorly member to some friends where she would be better looked after. It was decided that this should be paid out of the Poor Fund.

The minister in the Normanton section from September 1922 was Revd Ernest Warner and Mr Kappes was appointed Circuit Steward in the Rothwell Circuit.

In April 1923 it was reported that the father of the Society Steward for St Johns, a Mr Enos Nott, a retired railway signalman had died and a letter of condolence was sent to the family.

A letter was received from the Normanton Baptist minister suggesting the formation of a committee to deal with matters that needed concerted action from local churches. This committee was to be convened in April.

Mr Warner was unable to find anyone to replace Mr Nott as Society Steward at St Johns and the Leaders decided to call a special meeting to see if they could help the St Johns congregation to make their Sunday evening services brighter and more helpful to the young people.

CHAPTER SEVEN

Land, Buildings and Debt

The 1923 Annual Trustees Meeting at Upper Altofts was chaired by the new minister Revd E. Warner although the Superintendent was present. Revd Warner continued to do so throughout his tenure

The first mention of the cause of the problem with the extension land appears at this time. Mr Stephenson had been trying to see Sir Matthew regarding his wish "to preserve a right of way of entrance across the church land".

In the light of the previous subsidence problems it is perhaps surprising that the church granted Pope and Pearson mineral rights over two seams of coal under the whole of the church property. Nonetheless this was granted for the sum of £32.

The unrest at Normanton had not entirely gone and in February 1924 two members, Mr Harris and Mr Blakely, proposed that a special leaders meeting be held with the Superintendent to discuss the question of reverting to the Wakefield Circuit or of forming a circuit based on Normanton. This proposal was carried but in a Special Leaders Meeting in April a new proposal that "having carefully considered the question of division of the circuit the meeting does not feel that it can recommend any change" was adopted.

This meeting also considered the situation at St Johns and suggested that the Superintendent should make arrangements to adapt the Sunday evening service to the needs of the young people and to conduct a monthly week night service in a similar manner. It would seem that St Johns was attracting some young people.

Unfortunately the delegates appointed in February to attend the meeting to arrange an ecumenical committee had all been unable to attend and it was not until January 1925 that delegates to the new Local Church Council were elected.

Again there was no candidate for Society Steward at St Johns and Mr Warner proposed Mr Frederick Nott be appointed again which was carried.

In July of 1924 a new scheme of renovation was carried out at Upper Altofts. The walls were to receive three coats of paint and the frieze was to be redone in three colours in an original and exclusive design. A text (not specified) was to be written in a scroll behind the pulpit. This work was to be done at a cost of £20

September brought a new minister and a discussion about ministerial appointments. The minister was Revd Albert E. Burton, who had travelled for some 27 years, starting as a minister in the United Methodist Church. The conversations regarding ministerial appointments concluded that the Normanton minister should occupy the pulpit five Sundays out of the seven ministerial appointments in each quarter. This raises the question as to whether the lack of ministerial appointments was because of a perceived absence of their own minister or total ministerial appointments?

Revd Burton walked into a major problem at Altofts also. The land the church had bought for expansion (building a Sunday School) was still empty and considerable damage was being done to the church windows by people using the land as a playground. The Leaders Meeting negotiated the boundary with Mr Hailstone and fenced the land off, building two gates into the fence. Promptly, Mr Leake, property agent for Sir M. Dodsworth, demanded the opening of the large gate and had a load of rubbish dumped in the gateway blocking its closure. This seems a rather high handed way of resolving a dispute. Mr Hailstone advised that the rubbish was removed and the gate should be locked again.

There were lengthy arguments with Mr Leake regarding the fence and a right of way which Sir M. Dodsworth demanded from Church Road to the land at the rear. After considerable efforts the church consulted a solicitor, Sir William Middlesbrook of Leeds, and it became clear that there was indeed a right of way over the land. Sir M. Dodsworth asked for a 30 ft right of way which would have made the project not viable. The church offered 15 ft and had to settle for 20 ft which they felt was unfair. This right of way and the ownership of the land it crosses has been a matter of some disagreement ever since.

There were questions raised regarding the suitability and conduct of the caretaker as some dissatisfaction had been expressed regarding the way her duties were carried out. No resolution to the problem is recorded and some time later she asked to be relieved of her duties as her health made it difficult to fulfil them.

Electric light was becoming more common and Wakefield Road Wesleyan, in April 1927, discussed a proposal to install it. The agreed process was that the church should be asked to raise £350 to cover the cost of installing the electric light and clearing the church overdraft: a prudent scheme. The final decision was to require the trustees to draw up a definite scheme for church and school separately.

Miss Nixon came to the Wakefield Road Leaders Meeting with a request for the use of the Guild Room or another room on a Saturday afternoon. The Girls' League wished to do "something more definite for the crippled children of the town". The meeting promised Miss Nixon the use of a room.

The February meeting particularly thanked the ladies of the congregation for providing hospitality for preachers and three members, not named, for conveying preachers to appointments. This was a fairly new concept as preachers had usually made their own way in the past, often walking long distances. That there were three members willing to undertake this task suggests a growing spread of car ownership and some affluence in the congregation. After the meeting a faith supper was held. This is the first time the term is used in the local records, all previous entertainments having been provided by the ladies of the congregation.

The Ladies Sewing Society and its Sewing Meeting teas had been a useful source of financial aid to Wakefield Road but the meeting seems to have lapsed and, in 1928, Mr Nixon proposed that the ladies be asked to restart the meetings.

Although this is not yet reckoned to be the period of the Great Depression, unemployment in the North East was the highest in England at 15.1%, only Wales being higher. Revd Frank Rowley arrived into an area with severe poverty and unemployment in the mining industry all around. The membership, judging by the Trustees, were more likely to be affluent. They were largely shopkeepers, managers or railwaymen in the better jobs such as signalmen.

In November Mr Rowley received an appeal from the Yorkshire Evening Post "Boots for Bairns Fund". This had been in existence since the early 20s and continued to make appeals until the advent of the War. Mr Rowley responded by offering to do a slide show to raise funds for the appeal. At the next meeting, December, he reported that he had received £10 from Connexional funds and expected a parcel of clothing which was to be distributed at Normanton, Altofts, Stanley and Oulton.

A new venture was begun at Normanton at the beginning of 1929, Mrs Hinchcliffe and Miss Brighton formed a Girl Guides troop and Brownie pack with themselves as leaders.

The Leaders Meeting also asked that a letter be sent to Mr Blakely to record the very high regard in which he was held owing to his many years service at St Johns. This was linked with his retirement from the post of Senior Steward, thereafter stepping back into the role after a colleague's ill health.

Altofts now were in a position to build the new hall and school they had planned for some time. The finance committee put a maximum of £1,800 on the contract as this was what was in hand. Mr Hailstone was the architect appointed and after receiving several tenders he renegotiated the tender from Fenton of Tingley to a price of £1782 0s 5d, a remarkably precise figure for such a squeezed price.

Towards the end of the year Altofts received a letter from the Local Preacher's Secretary asking that the time of the morning service be moved from 10.30 to 10.45 as this would be of great help to those conveying preachers. Presumably this was to stagger the service times in the section but it must have meant that the drivers remained at the service to which they last delivered a preacher. After some discussion a vote was taken and this arrangement was accepted.

Speaking at the Altofts Annual Meeting, Mr Rowley commented on what he saw as a lack of missionary spirit and he proposed cottage and open air meetings. This was agreed. It had been some years since Altofts had held a Love Feast. As a corollary to this move the following proposal was put to the Trustees: that the notice board should have on it "all seats free. Visitors welcome", that the gallery should be shut for Sunday morning services, the children sit at the front and suitable sidesmen be appointed to welcome people to the service. One of Mr Rowley's first acts in arriving had been to suggest that the Normanton Choir should sing in some of the streets around the church as "this would possibly do a lot of good". Although that was agreed there are no reports of the outcome.

Mr Blackburn of Normanton had been Plan Secretary for some years and the Altofts Leaders proposed that he should no longer be responsible for filling the blank days on the plan and that the two ministers should make the plan together. There is no rationale offered for this change in a long standing practice but it may be that Altofts had been unhappy with Mr Blackburn's appointees.

The trustees of Altofts manse were granted permission to sell the manse and purchase one in Normanton when the opportunity arose. Circumstances, and uncertainties of the following years, meant this never happened.

September 1930 brought the report of the death of Mr George W. Denton a long standing member of Wakefield Road and of the Rothwell Circuit, having been treasurer in the beginning and choirmaster at Normanton for many years.

The new building at Altofts was completed although there was still considerable work to be done on furnishings.

The Rothwell Wesleyan Circuit appointed Mr T. Young as their representative to the 1931 Methodist Congress held in Sheffield to discuss Methodist Union. It was losing both its ministers that year and the invitation committee met to decide on the two ministers to be invited. Revd Allen Holt had agreed to accept their invitation to come as Superintendent and two names were suggested as the second minister. Neither were to accept the situation, but it may be of interest to today's readers that one of those was Revd F. Pratt Green, the hymn writer. The meeting reported a membership of 470 with 50 on trial and 117 junior members.

In 1931 the Normanton Permanent Orchestra requested the use of the Sunday School from 7.30 to 10 p.m. every Friday for 12 months. After discussion, the Trustees Meeting confirmed the secretary's action in not granting the use of the premises.

At the beginning of 1931 Rothwell circuit was still carrying debt and the finance committee discussed holding a garden party to reduce it. Perhaps because a garden party would have meant deferring the matter for some months or because this had not proved to be a productive strategy in recent times, it was decided to make a special assessment on each of the churches and the sums allocated were £10 to Rothwell and Normanton, £5 to Stanley and Altofts and £2 10s to Woodlesford, Oulton and Carlton. St Johns and Ouzlewell Green were asked to contribute what they could.[22]

In September the circuit received two new ministers, the Superintendent was Revd A. Holt of Castleford and Revd Edmund Thompson came to the Normanton section. The membership of the circuit at this time was 537.

Unity Discussions

Methodist Union was now a reality, although what sort of reality was still to be seen. The March meeting opened with a talk from Edmund Thompson about the coming changes and the circuit appointed three members from Normanton to be part of the Normanton Methodist Council. While this section of the Rothwell circuit seemed to be keen to move on and become part of something new, the rest of the circuit was less keen. The largest church, Rothwell, was not even prepared to contemplate an agreement with the ex-Prim church in the town, perhaps being close neighbours was a hindrance, although this did not seem to trouble the two churches in Wakefield Road, Normanton.

In December letters were read out from the Prims in Rothwell, Leeds East and Normanton regarding reorganisation. A long discussion took place but the general feeling was that the matter could not be hurried. It was also decided that they could not make individual arrangements but must consider the whole area. Looking back, the time it took for local circuits to reorganise seems remarkable, but what was happening at Rothwell seems not to have been

---

[22] These sums seem tiny to us today, but since the total raised would have the spending power of over £1,600 today this was not an insignificant amount to raise.

uncommon. There seems never to have been any intention for all of the churches in the circuit to move in one direction. Normanton had always been uncomfortable in that circuit and Altofts too was much closer to the churches in the Normanton circuit than to Rothwell although even here the Leaders' Meeting took the decision at the March 1933 meeting to leave the matter over until the committee, formed to discuss the matter, reported in June. Were that to happen the Rothwell ex-Wesleyan circuit would lose almost half its membership and could not be seen as viable. Unfortunately the Rothwell people seemed totally unwilling to contemplate creating their own union locally. This reluctance was to derail the process for many years to come.

This new year also saw Altofts lose its choirmaster of 40 years, Mr J. R. Eccles, who was retiring owing to poor health. The Stewards asked Mr C. B. Carrington to fill the role until the next Trustees meeting. Mr Carrington was to be confirmed in the role at that time.

In June a letter from the Normanton Leaders' Meeting was read out at the Rothwell Quarterly Meeting asking that St Johns should become a charge on the circuit. It was decided to form a committee to investigate the matter but this was not resolved quickly.

The Union proposals again took up some considerable time at this meeting and the decision was taken, on the proposal of Mr Hailstone, to refer it back to each church to find their view on the matter. Although the Circuit Secretary, Mr Hailstone was a member at Altofts and perhaps hoped that the views of the churches might prevail, this was always treated as a circuit matter.

With the possible upheaval of Union still in mind, Mr Hailstone drew attention to the new legislation regarding ministerial appointments and proposed that the two ministers should be asked to remain for a fourth year. This was greeted with applause.

Nothing had been decided about St Johns but a special collection was taken up at the December Quarterly Meeting to try to clear their debt. Yet another committee was appointed to explore the question of Union and to meet with the other parties in April.

Normanton seem to have been becoming impatient, as a letter from their Leaders' Meeting was read at the March 1934 Quarterly Meeting asking that "Union be consummated as soon as possible" The Circuit Steward, Mr Humphrey spoke on the difficulties ahead and suggested that they should move very carefully in the matter. The Normanton members, Mr Kappes, Mr Blackburn and Mr Johnson, along with Revd Thompson spoke in favour of the Normanton resolution. A general discussion took place at the meeting and it was proposed that the committee elected to attend the joint meeting in April explore the case further and report back at the June meeting.

There was no report from the June meeting and between then and September, Revd Allen Holt died suddenly. The Invitation committee asked Revd Edmund Thompson to become Superintendent, moving to the Rothwell manse and to ask the President to find a suitable man for Normanton at a salary of £250 per annum.

Union plans were pretty much put aside at the September meeting. After what is described as "a long and fairly representative discussion" with Mr Humphrey, Mr Isam, Mr Hodgson and Mr Seanor speaking about the difficulties and suggesting that the financial part was impossible, a proposal was made by Mr Humphrey and Mrs Hutchinson that the scheme stand over for five years. An amendment from Mr Young and Mr Johnson that the scheme be referred back to each church for further discussion was defeated. The final vote that the original scheme be put aside was carried by 30 votes to six.

Carrying on

Altofts bought 180 of the new 1933 *Methodist Hymn Books* including 30 music editions at a total cost of £31 10s and Mr G. A. Jackson, the preacher on November 11th, was asked if he would curtail the service so that the choir could lead the singing of hymns from the new book.

At the beginning of the year a meeting was called to appoint new Trustees for Altofts as, owing to death and resignations, there were now insufficient for the duties. The following were appointed:

Claude Bramley Carrington, Farmer
Arthur Senior, Miner
George Newsome, Colliery engineman
James Benton, Grocer
Albert Macdonald , Miner
Walter Eccles, Dairyman
Bernard Arthur Shaw, Clerk[23]
Aaron Plant, Miner
James Arthur Berridge, Miner
Jack Firth, Clerk
Norman Eric England, Colliery Surveyor
Stephen Reuben West, Railway Foreman

---

[23] Arthur Shaw, who was only 21 at this time, was also a local preacher and shortly after this, he was called to the ministry. Training at Richmond College he entered the ministry in 1941 and served as an RAF chaplain from 1942 until the end of the war. Arthur was Chair of the Chester and Stoke district and in 1977, President of Conference. He died suddenly in 1988

During 1935, Normanton Wesleyan Church underwent a total renovation with cleaning, redecoration and external pointing.

The Rothwell Quarterly Meeting in March 1935 is able to greet Revd James R. McNeal and his wife Violet. Revd McNeal was the President's appointee and the minister at Normanton. Sadly, the meeting also had to express their sympathy for the passing of his father who had also been a minister.

Normanton seem still to have been unhappy with their lot as there was a discussion about the fact that Normanton had only contributed £45 that quarter. This drop of £10 seems to have been a deliberate omission as there was a discussion about the merits of their argument. In the end Mr Johnson agreed to consult the Normanton Leaders Meeting to obtain their consent to forward the omitted sum.

An enquiry was made regarding the committee formed in June two years previously to look into the conditions at St Johns. It seems the committee had not met "because no one had taken the initiative to call a meeting".

Both these matters come to the next meeting. The treasurer, Mr Hailstone, reported that the £10 due from the previous quarter from Normanton had still not been received and that he had been informed by the Normanton people that they would decide about this at the end of their financial year. The Circuit had decided to make an application to Home Missions for a grant for St Johns. This application was declined.

Rothwell again decided that, owing to the unresolved question of circuit rearrangements, it would be unwise to change both ministers at the same time and Mr Thompson was invited to stay until 1937, but the new minister Mr McNeal was asked to change at the end of 1936.

The Altofts Leaders' Meeting discussed the re-forming of a scout troop, but there had been difficulties previously with damage and disorder and this still caused concern. After a lengthy discussion a list of conditions was created including that there should be suitable leaders with a connection to the church. If these were fulfilled permission woud be granted.

Despite the previous decision a cheque for £25 was received from Home Missions for St Johns in December 1935.

In June a party of students from Cliff College made a visit to Normanton and the work they did there was much appreciated. Revd Thompson read an appeal to the Quarterly Meeting from the Convocation of the Wesley Deaconess Order for 25s being the Rothwell share of the District debt of £32 towards the cost of Convocation.

James McNeal was replaced in 1936 by a minister from Cornwall, Revd R. Tudno-Davies who started on a salary of £270. The invitation committee decided to invite him to be Superintendent from 1938 but he asked for time to decide. In March 1938 they received his answer. He declined both the superintendency and the invitation to remain as second minister owing to failing health. He left the circuit in 1938 and was called to higher service in 1941.

Throughout 1937 there were considerable efforts to find the £105 due by Altofts to Leeds Methodist Council for repairs and alterations to the buildings. The final £20 was proving very hard to fund. One fund raising example illustrates the difficulty. The choir of St Paul's Methodist Church in Brighouse offered a concert for which they would provide their own expenses. Despite selling 155 tickets and 53 programmes the concert only raised £5.

In June 1938, at his last Quarterly Meeting, Revd Thompson introduced the matter of the Performing Rights Society and informed the meeting that a fee of £2 12s 6d would cover all the churches for a year.

The Revd Arthur P. Shorter was appointed as minister in the Normanton section from 1938 but with a salary of £250, this would relate to his years of travel. The new superintendent was the Revd H. Ashby.

Altofts' problems with the Leeds Methodist Council debt were resolved in February 1939 with the arrival of a cheque from Mr Rank. The treasurer was able to report that a cheque had been sent to the Leeds Methodist Council. Unfortunately their financial troubles were far from over. A letter was received at the same meeting informing them that they had been assessed at £35 towards the cost of manse repairs and also that there was a serious deficit, which had accumulated over the previous two years, regarding assessments.

Normanton Urban District Council had approached the Wakefield Road stewards regarding using the Sunday School as a Casualty Clearing Station in case of war. The Trustees, on the proposal of Mr Blackburn and Mr Kappes, agreed to this use for the schoolroom.

Mr Blackburn asked the meeting to consider the legacy left by the late Robert Blackburn Hirst saying that it was the wish of Mrs Marsden that the legacy should go toward the purchase of a caretaker's house. He said that he himself would contribute £50 towards this. The meeting proposed and agreed that the money should be deposited with the Halifax Building Society until the trustees authorised its withdrawal for this purpose. Mr Blackburn too kept his promise and sent a cheque for £50 to be used for the same purpose. In the event, the money remained on deposit for a considerable time until it was used for other purposes.

In the autumn, with the declaration of war, a meeting was called at Altofts to explain the new lighting regulations and the need to make arrangements for the concealing of lights at a 6 p.m. service. This being so, the circuit plan had been made with all evening services rescheduled for 3.30 p.m. Altofts declined to accept this and decided that they would continue to hold services at 6 p.m. The superintendent explained that, as the preachers had been informed of the new time, they would have to make arrangements with the preachers, especially any not able to make the 6 p.m. time. This seems to have been the response at Normanton also as Mr Ashby informed the Circuit Quarterly Meeting that all evening services would be held in the afternoon with the exception of Normanton and Altofts.

In 1941 the Altofts organist resigned, Mrs Gaspar, nee Hailstone was moving to South America with her husband. Miss Iley Carrington was asked to take the post and agreed for a short time which became a regular post at £3 per annum. Miss Carrington's reluctance was clarified at the end of 1942 when she resigned to enter the nursing profession.

Despite the obvious wartime strictures, arrangements were made to celebrate the Altofts centenary during September 18th-27th 1942. These would take place with a new minister as Revd William McCormack Myles came from Bristol to live with his wife Elsie at Patience Lane in September 1942. Mr Myles was to remain until 1945 but when, in 1944 he received the invitation, he told the committee that he had been instructed by his doctor that he should not travel to the more distant parts of the circuit, which must have put a burden on his colleague.

At Normanton, the schoolroom, which had been suggested as a Casualty Clearing station was in fact being used as a Labour Exchange. The Trustees Minutes record several complaints about heating from the manager of the Labour Exchange.

The Circuit Steward, Mr Hodgson had written to the Altofts Society Steward to remind him that they had been paying £2 10s short on their Circuit assessment of £25 for the last four quarters leaving them £10 in debt to the circuit. The trustees decided that they were not able to pay that at present. By February 1943, the debt to the circuit had risen to £26 and the finance committee wrote to the Trustees stating that they were unable to pay this and requesting the Trustees' help. The Trustees agreed to pay the £26. Unlike in the past, this was not personal payment. The minutes of the meeting showed that the Trust Funds held a balance of £58 17s 1p in the bank.

The 1943 meeting appointed a number of new officers including Claude Carrington as secretary as well as choir master and Mrs Cyril Taffinder as organist.

In June 1944 the committee set up to consider the condition of St Johns at last reported and recommended the closure of St Johns as it was in such a poor condition.

September brought more financial problems. A discussion was held at the Circuit Quarterly Meeting regarding ministerial stipends. It was stated that the cost of living had increased by 75% since pre-war days and suggested a minimum for superintendents of £280, a minister who had travelled 20 years £270 and one who had travelled 10 years £260.[24] The possibility of a war bonus was mooted, but the treasurer pointed out that the circuit was already £100 in debt.

December produced new assessments for all the churches, doubtless as a consequence in the rise needed for ministerial stipends. The quarterly figures were: Rothwell £62, Normanton £55 Altofts £28, Stanley £21, Woodlesford £14, Carlton £8, Ouzlewell Green £4.

The circuit had negotiated a visit from the Home Missions Caravan Hope, staffed by two Deaconesses, which had visited Normanton. The meeting heard that it had been a great success with the formation of a Junior Guild.

In March 1945 Mr Hailstone reported to the circuit that the building at St Johns had been sold for £76 and the cash handed to the Normanton Trust Treasurer.[25]

---

[24] The average pay for a building trades craftsman at this time would be £255 per annum and a labourer could expect to earn £205.

[25] Although monies for the sale of a redundant church are the property of the circuit, the St Johns building had been paid for and maintained by Normanton as a local project.

1945 again brought a change in both ministers with Revd T Clifford Brown coming as superintendent and Laurence Larter to the Normanton section to live at Patience Lane with his wife Hilda, remaining until long after amalgamation.

March 1946 brought conflicting news regarding the Carrington family. The meeting expressed sympathy at the death of Mr Thomas Carrington and congratulated Miss Iley Carrington, daughter of Claude the organist and a Trustee at Altofts, on being accepted to go to Deaconess Training College at Ilkley. Two years later she was ordained at Manchester and went on to do language training in Paris before being sent to the Ivory Coast. In 1953 she was to marry a Methodist Minister Antony Hearle which meant her leaving the Order.

Changes in the Normanton Trustees during 1946 and the attendance at meetings show the dominance of three families. The Kappes and Cresseys were related and between them they had three members on the trustees and the Blackburns also had three members. These were some of the more regular and active at the Trustee meetings.

In January 1947 the Altofts Annual Meeting received the resignation of Mr T. H. Hailstone as treasurer owing to ill health. He had served the church and circuit over many years. He was replaced by Mr Eccles.

An unusual entry appears in these minutes:

"owing to the non-acceptance of the Methodist Rules and Regulations by a section of our people, it was decided to inform them that in future our premises would not be available for the holding of the monthly devotional services.

CHAPTER EIGHT

Amalgamation at last

The first intimation in the minutes of the imminent amalgamation appears in the Trustees Minutes of the Normanton Wesleyan Church. Revd Laurence Larter outlined the plans and Mr Johnson and Mr Harry Blackburn spoke strongly in favour, but it was thought there was insufficient detail. It was resolved that the whole scheme should be brought again for the Trustees to consider. The Trustees minutes do not refer to the matter again.

For the ex-Primitive Normanton Methodist Circuit, things went morre smoothly. In February 1947 Revd Hall outlined to the Normanton Quarterly Meeting the proposal of a scheme for amalgamation of the Wakefield Road Church and the Upper Altofts Church with the Normanton Circuit. It was recommended that this proposal be accepted.

In March 1947, the Rothwell circuit again discussed boundaries. The proposal that Rothwell ex-Wesleyans amalgamate with Rothwell ex Primitive was discussed and again Mr Hodgson and Mr Seanor spoke against the proposal saying that it was not practicable in the immediate future. The proposal was defeated by a vote of 2 for and 30 against.

For the first time there was little opposition to the desire of Normanton and Altofts to join with the Normanton ex-Primitive circuit. The proposal to do so was carried by a majority vote. These decisions were confirmed at the July Conference.

At a series of meetings to iron out one or two of the details of the amalgamation, it was agreed that any application from Rothwell for compensation for property should be repudiated. This was in particular a reference to the Altofts manse occupied by Revd Laurence Larter who was to join the new circuit. Perhaps surprisingly for this period, Russell Hall owned a car and it was agreed as part of the amalgamation arrangements to pay him 50 shillings a quarter for the use of his car within the circuit. This would replace travel allowance as paid at the time.

In Rothwell the matter of the Altofts manse was viewed somewhat differently. Mr Blackburn of Normanton said that he hoped a fair and just compensation be paid for the manse.

In the end, the September Rothwell meeting had a proposal that £70 which had been raised in Altofts for the manse fund should be refunded to Normanton but this proposal was defeated. It was decided that this money should be retained but no compensation should be sought for the loss of the Altofts manse. This decision may have been swayed by the difficulty of deciding a value for a manse with a considerable debt still in place.

The agreement was placed before the meeting and with 28 members present there was a vote in favour of 27 with one against. A celebration of the amalgamation was to be held in September.

The first Circuit meeting of the newly formed Normanton Methodist Circuit took place in Wakefield Road and was attended by both ministers and representatives from all the churches. The membership returns were agreed as follows:

Normanton Primitive Circuit	325
Wakefield Road	112
Upper Altofts	56
Total	481

The meeting agreed to support Trinity's application for a loan of £400, but there is no indication as to what this was for. An application by Upper Altofts for a loan to purchase a cottage for the caretaker was supported. It was stated that the cottage was to cost half price because of the kindly action of the late Mr Hailstone who had made such an offer to the Trustees. Although a fund for this purpose appears in the schedules for years after amalgamation, the purchase is not recorded.

Following usual practice, a sum of £60 per annum was agreed as manse rents to be paid quarterly in equal amounts. This was to fund the debt on the manses not for maintenance.

The final act of this first meeting was a sad duty. Mr Hall read out a letter from the Connexional Chapel Committee regarding Castleford Road. This gave a decision about the demolition of the church and the disposal of the furnishings and equipment. Mr Baines, the Society steward, made an earnest plea for the continuation of the present Society, but this time the response was to set up a committee to "get on with the job" and report back. After a continuing struggle, the demolition finally took place in early 1950 although the land remained on the schedules for at least another ten years.

Shortly after this, Mr Hailstone offered to sell the cottage occupied by the Upper Altofts caretaker, Mrs F Marshall, to the Altofts Trust for £100. Revd Larter and Mr Carrington were delegated to look after this. Between then and the next meeting in July, Mr Hailstone passed away and Mr Carrington reported that Mrs Hailstone was still keen that her husband's wishes should be carried out. The meeting unanimously decided that Mr Carrington should carry on with the negotiations. There is never any explanation and the cottage does not seem to change hands at this time. Mrs Mary Carrington, wife of Claude's son Raymond has told me that the cottage came into the possession of the church, but later was the subject of a compulsory purchase order when only £50 was received from the Council.

The celebrations

The amalgamation formally took place on 1st September 1947 as the two ex-Wesleyan churches of Wakefield Road and Upper Altofts joined with the seven churches of the ex-Primitive Circuit to become the Normanton Methodist Circuit. As part of the celebrations, there were special services throughout September and the rest of that quarter. On Saturday September 6th there was a Welcome Service at Trinity, a Celebration Meeting of the new circuit at Wakefield Road on Monday, September 8th, a United Celebration Meeting Sharlston Common on Saturday the 13th and a Grand Women's Rally completed the September events.

All of these events were presided over by the two ministers, Revd Russell Hall Superintendent of the circuit and Revd Laurence Larter

"Our union should strengthen us for our witness and work, and make more effective the evangelising of our town and its neighbourhood. It will do so, if with adventurous faith, we all give ourselves whole-heartedly to the fulfilment of that aim.

Good-will and patience will also be required, and a sacrificial willingness to set aside any preferences and customs which in the past marked our division."

CHAPTER NINE

Hope, Struggle and Change

At the time of the amalgamation the churches of the Normanton circuit were at the peak of their strength and vitality. The following twenty years were, unfortunately, a period of gradual decline. This was part of a general trend in the Connexion and, despite valiant efforts, the circuit and the district were looking at plans for new direction by the end of the 1950s.

It is difficult to pinpoint the start of this decline. Beckbridge had managed to pay the debt on their buildings by the end of 1949 under the ministry of the Revd Campion Wright. They had appointed 14 new trustees as Samuel Mapplethorpe was the only remaining original trustee. Trinity had engaged in building work at the time of the amalgamation and the circuit seemed strong.

By 1963 the Revd Dr Edward Baguley had instigated talks in the Circuit based on the belief that the Circuit would be better served if the two churches in Wakefield Road were to join together, saving building costs and offering a stronger society. The following year, after experimenting with joint morning services at Trinity the two societies agreed to widen that experience into monthly joint services and in December 1964 the joint trustees meeting of Wesley and Trinity agreed unanimously that the two societies should amalgamate and that Wesley should be sold and some of the proceeds used to repair the exterior of Trinity.

Beckbridge had also found themselves with problems and in 1964, they raised the possibility of joining with Hopetown. This was not agreed and the church was faced with dealing with damp rot and dry rot. A district planning commission had proposed that Beckbridge should do the repairs and continue as a place of worship but the Society found themselves unable to face the work and told the Circuit they wished to close and to join with the two central churches. Dr Baguley then had a meeting with Hopetown, which had transferred to the Normanton Circuit from Castleford in 1958,to ask them to consider joining with the other churches in the joint venture. Hopetown replied that this was a matter for the Trustees. It appears that the original Trustees were no longer available and a new set was elected. This new Trustees Meeting decided that they could not agree to the amalgamation and decided to carry on as they were.

In September 1965 Wesley and Trinity churches united as one congregation. Wesley was sold for £4,000 and the new Society, to include the Beckbridge Congregation, was renamed Normanton Methodist Church. The memberships involved give a clue as to the driving force behind the change. Trinity brought 78, Wesley 61, and Beckbridge 22, a total of 123, a loss of 38 members 24 of whom had ceased to meet owing to the amalgamation. This sort of loss is seen in most such amalgamations. More telling is the drop in membership since 1947 with Wesley losing half its membership and the Circuit reducing from 481 to 380 over the period. One of the factors taken into account by the Joint Trustees Meeting when considering the merger was that Normanton had seating for 1500 people in the two churches.

The Circuit Finance Committee met in October 1965 to discuss the assessments. There was concern expressed regarding the burden this placed on the members and Mr C. B. Carrington suggested that Home Missions be approached for a grant towards the cost of the second minister. Mr C. Shearn and Mr. W. Seymour proposed that the previous minute regarding an invitation for a second minister be rescinded and the Circuit petition the District Committee to have a minister withdrawn in September 1966. This was agreed.

The following year was one of dramatic decisions and turnarounds. In May a letter was received from Streethouse regarding a move to Pontefract Circuit. It seems that Pontefract was willing and a decision was made to ask permission of the District Committee for the move to go ahead.

The Circuit was reminded at the June meeting that Mr Gameson, the minister in Normanton would leave in September. Despite the previous decision, a probationer, the Revd Geoffrey Hunter was stationed in Normanton and a Home Missions grant of £1000 was forthcoming.

In the meantime the District Planning Committee had been considering matters in the whole of the area and had come forward with some proposals. The suggestion was that Streethouse, New Sharlston and Sharlston Common should join Pontefract and Normanton and Altofts join with Castleford. The Quarterly Meeting agreed to a proposal by Mr C. Ransome and Mr W. Baines that the Circuit should stay as they were. There were problems in Castleford and the amalgamations fell through. From that point on Normanton faced serious financial problems, particularly around maintaining two ministers.

In 1968 this had clearly been resolved in the only way it could, the Circuit agreeing to the sale of both manses and to buy a single manse in Station Road at a cost of £4,500. This would mean the loss of a minister. Geoffrey Hunter left in 1969 and was not replaced. Dr Edward Baguley, who had been in the Circuit for six years left at the same time to be replaced by Revd James Gaskell, who would be the first resident of Station Road, although Patience Lane did not sell until 1970. At this point the membership had reduced to 288.

Hopetown now found itself in great difficulty. The Borough Council had produced plans to build a new industrial estate on the edge of town and Cooperative Street and all the houses to Loscoe were to come down. Despite strong representations by Mr Gaskell the Council would make no offer for the church buildings and it was clear that closure was the only option. Mr A. Boulton reluctantly proposed the closure and sale of the church. This was seconded by Mrs S. Parkinson and the meeting decided to close in 1972 with a transfer of members to Normanton. The Normanton Church Council expressed some disquiet about the difficulties some members would have in getting to church from Hope Town and a rota of cars was arranged to aid this.

The Circuit General Purposes Meeting in February 1971 received a report from the minister, Revd Gaskell, about the situation in the Circuit. He explained that, not only was there a shortage of trained local preachers, but a shortage of lay officials. Overseas Missions, Home Missions, Christian Stewardship, Women's Work, Women's Fellowship and Youth Work were all without officers which meant he had little time for pastoral work and mission. The meeting expressed fears for the future of Methodism.

At the March Quarterly Meeting Revd Gaskell was invited to remain another two years. This would have taken him up to retirement and was doubtless meant kindly, but Mr Gaskell came to the June meeting declining to accept the extension. All attempts to reorganise the Circuit had fallen through and the shortage of lay leadership had perhaps daunted him. He left the Circuit in September 1972 to be replaced by Revd Owen R. Johnson who was to remain until 1976.

At the June 1973 meeting, Mr C. B. Carrington retired after serving as circuit steward for 23 years. Mr Johnson instigated a discussion regarding uniting with other circuits but was told that opinion was divided on the matter. He made the interesting decision to ask that the matter be dropped for the duration of his ministry amongst them.

Conference had decreed that the next meeting would be called the Circuit Meeting rather than the Quarterly Meeting and Mr Stephen Furness was appointed Circuit Meeting secretary. The membership in the circuit was now only 246 and the assessment was set at £3 per member per quarter.

The District was now more concerned than ever and, in 1978, the District Chair organised a meeting with the Superintendents of Castleford, Normanton and Pontefract. Castleford seem to have been unwilling to make changes but in August 1979, the new minister, Revd J. Clifford Adams presided over the last meeting of the Normanton Circuit. Present was Revd R. Berry, the Pontefract minister, who explained the administrative setup in the Pontefract Circuit and welcomed Mr Furness as Junior Assistant Finance Secretary Steward in the new circuit.

Despite the Centenary Celebrations in 1942, Normanton had become an independent circuit for the first time in 1879 which gives exactly 100 years of independent life for the Normanton Primitive/Methodist Circuit.

APPENDICES

1. THE CHURCHES

The history of the Circuit would not be complete without a brief account of the churches which have made it up. Most of these churches are no longer in existence, but they all contributed to the history and growth of the Circuit.

EX- PRIMITIVE METHODISTS

Trinity (Wakefield Road)

The first building was a small wooden Chapel built, in 1868, on leased land in Woodhouse. The site was later the Woodhouse School and the building now houses various commercial enterprises.

By 1874 this chapel was found to be too small and the land where the present church stands was bought. The original church building cost £1442. The schoolroom was built in the same year at a cost of £700. Another eight classrooms were added to the school in 1894 at a cost of £300, which included a new heating system. As the congregation grew, further additions were made. In 1904 an infant school was attached to the school and the whole chapel was remodelled to provide a worship area capable of seating 450 people. This stage of the building was the most expensive, costing £2000. The organ was installed a year later at a cost £350, half of which was contributed by Andrew Carnegie.

Beckbridge

This was originally a mission work of the Circuit until, in 1885, a wooden Chapel and Sunday School was built just below the site of the later brick church. It only cost £80 but it could seat 150 people.

Ten years later the Circuit strengthened the Society in Beckbridge by sending members from various churches in the Circuit. This was clearly effective as by 1899 they were able to build the brick church which still stands in Castleford Road, although, sadly, now a furniture workshop. The original cost was £1400. The classroom at the rear of the church was added later.

Castleford Road

The church in Castleford Road was built in 1897 as a replacement for a smaller church and schoolroom in Foxbridge Row. Hopetown Primitive Methodist had been part of the Pontefract Circuit, growing from house meetings in Whitwood into a strong Society. The Foxbridge Row church was built in 1870 as the Society grew in strength. Shortly after moving to Castleford Road the Society moved to the Castleford Circuit and then joined the Normanton Circuit in 1901. Still a thriving society they added a Central Hall, Primary department and eight classrooms to the building in 1903. In 1945 the Connexional Buildings Committee recommended that worship should cease as the building was in a hazardous condition owing to subsidence. The church was finally closed and demolished in 1950.

Lock Lane (Altofts)

The earliest Primitive Methodist worship in Altofts was outdoor services conducted in Good Hope Terrace. Eventually the group got the use of an old barn at the back of 'Greystones'. Later they were able to find some rooms in the centre of the village. In 1861 one of the members, Mr Norton, offered a room in his thatched cottage which stood where the Parish Hall now stands. Their next home was No. 2 Temple Place, which was to be their last temporary home. They worked to raise the money for a permanent church and in 1871 they were able to build the church in Lock Lane. This original building was extended and vestries added about 1907. The first of the vestries was built by one of the members, Mr J. Crane with the assistance of several other members. This church was to remain in use until 1989 when the new Altofts Church was opened.

New Sharlston

The chapel in New Sharlston was built by Crossley and Sons of Halifax in 1868 for the Colliery owners. It was leased to the Primitive Methodists in the village after a ballot of the worshippers. It was never the property of the Society or the circuit. A school was built in 1939, which was paid for by the local Society. Once a thriving church it struggled to maintain the buildings which led to the eventual closure in 1970. The NCB invoked the maintenance clause in the original lease agreement which permitted the ending of the tenancy.

Streethouse

1979

Originally services in Streethouse were held in the cottage of one of the members until the Society were able to get the use of a barn attached to Streethouse Farm which was owned by Mr H. Briggs. In 1879 land was bought from Mr Graves at 2s 6d a foot and the members of the society dug out the foundations themselves. The church was opened for worship the following year. In 1925 the Sunday School was built and the church underwent a series of improvements . The original building was demolished in 1994 and the schoolroom converted into a modern church.

Sharlston Common

The original place of worship, in 1879, was the house of Mr Jay. By 1881 the Society had grown to 20 members and was meeting in a cottage in Albert Terrace. The Society continued to grow and in 1889 they built a wooden chapel which was to serve them for 24 years. In 1902 the Society bought the land for the chapel from the Earl of Westmoreland and the specifications for the new building were prepared in 1912 by the Architect, W. Hamilton Fearnley, Station Lane, Featherstone, at which time they borrowed £550 from the Chapel Aid Association. This loan was to be paid back at the rate of £21 per annum, but in fact was repaid in full in 1942. The Chapel, on the main Wakefield Road (the present Weeland Road) was built in 1913 and did not close until 1980.

EX-WESLEYAN METHODIST

St Johns

As a place of worship this appears on the Primitive Methodist plan from at least 1878. The work seems to have been largely carried out from "a preaching house". There was a long- standing plan to build a mission chapel which never came to fruition.

In 1898 the work in St Johns was taken over by the Wesleyan Church in Wakefield Road who built a mission hut there in 1899. Despite being a constant struggle this remained in being until being sold in 1945.

Upper Altofts

Circa 1965

The church was built in 1842 on a piece of land bought from John Denison, a builder. Enlarged and renovated in 1865 the building was then gutted by fire in 1886 and completely renovated again at a cost of £361. In 1921 land was bought to build a separate schoolroom. This was started in 1929 and opened in 1930 with a large hall and extra rooms. This building was to remain until long after the circuit amalgamation in 1947. The Church was demolished in 1989 and the present church building was built on to the schoolroom in 1990.

Wakefield Road

The principal Wesleyan Church in the area was the home of the Normanton Society. Built in 1868 the original building was converted into a schoolroom and vestries in 1885 and a new and enlarged church build alongside the original at a cost of £1564. The organ was bought in 1901. Closed in 1965 the building still remains today.

EX-UNITED METHODIST

Hopetown

Pontefract Road, Hopetown was originally a United Methodist Free Church. In 1907 the UMFC, the Methodist New Connexion and the Bible Christians joined together as the United Methodist Church, continuing in that form until Methodist Union in 1932. Hopetown at that time was part of the Castleford UMFC circuit and became part of the Castleford Methodist Circuit. In 1958, under the ministry of the Revd J. Roberts, they decided to join the Normanton Circuit. In 1972 they were forced to close owing to the redevelopment of the Loscoe area into the new industrial estate.

2.   The Ministers and Manses

Primitive Methodist Ministers

No 3 The Grove

1879   T. Waite
1881   H. Crabtree
1883   P. T. Yarker
1887   W. Bennett
1888   B. Luddington
          B. Haddon
1889   A. McKechnie
1892   J. Binns
1895   J. Teece

No. 1 Freeston Terrace   356 Castleford Rd.
(39 Church Lane)

1896   J. Teece
1898   J. Bennett
1901   W. R. Fallas
1905   T. Dickinson   J. Palmer
1908   P. T. Yarker   W. Woodley
1912   T. H. Bryant   E. Reveley
1914   W. C. Tonks   W. R. Reed
1919   J. E. Leuty
1923   J. N. Clague
1926   J. T. Clarke
1930   W. Jacques
1936   R. Street
1941   C. Wacey
1945   R. Hall

Wesleyan Ministers (Rothwell Circuit)

In Lodgings

1892 H. Nicholls
1893 E. Coulson
1893 E. Bulmer

9 Patience Lane, Altofts

1896 J. T. Tyreman
1899 W. Salisbury
1902 R. Whitehead
1905 H. W. Pates
1908 A. Crawshaw
1911 M. Philipson
1914 J. Wilson
1918 W. J. Page
1922 E. Warner
1925 A. Burton
1928 F. Rowley
1931 E. Thompson
1934 J. R. McNeal
1936 R. T. Davies
1938 A. P. Shorter
1942 W. M. Myles
1945 L. Larter

Ministers After Amalgamation

Church Lane Manse	Patience Lane Manse
1947 R. Hall	1947 L. Larter
1948 A. Campion Wright	
1949	F. S. Morgan
1951 F. E. Wilson	F. S. Morgan (Super)
1953	Percy Robinson (Super)
1954 D. Horford	
1956 W. Hewison	J. McLoughlin (Super)
1959	A. Cushion (Super)
1960 Len Lord	
1962 B. J. Gameson	
1963	E. Baguley (Super)
1966 G. Hunter	
1968 Manse sold	1970 Manse Sold

Station Road Manse, 1969

1969 J. Gaskell
1972 O. Johnson
1976 C. Adams

24, Cambridge Street.
Castleford,
March 1886.

To the Authorities of the
Normanton Circuit,
Dear Brethren,
   I am instructed to inform
you that we accept the boundary
suggested by you (as marked
on the sketch plan forwarded)
between the two Circuits.

   By order and on behalf of the
Quarterly Meeting held March 1886

Joseph C. Livesey, Prest.

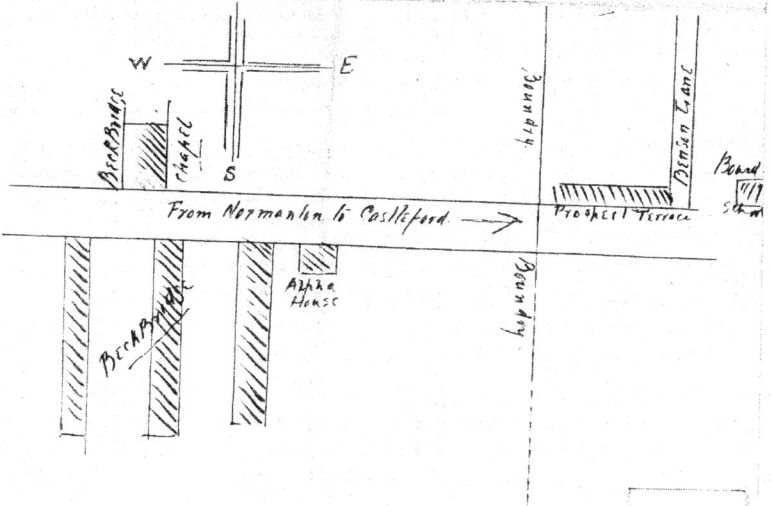

Schematic of
the Rothwell/Leeds

Wesleyan Circuit

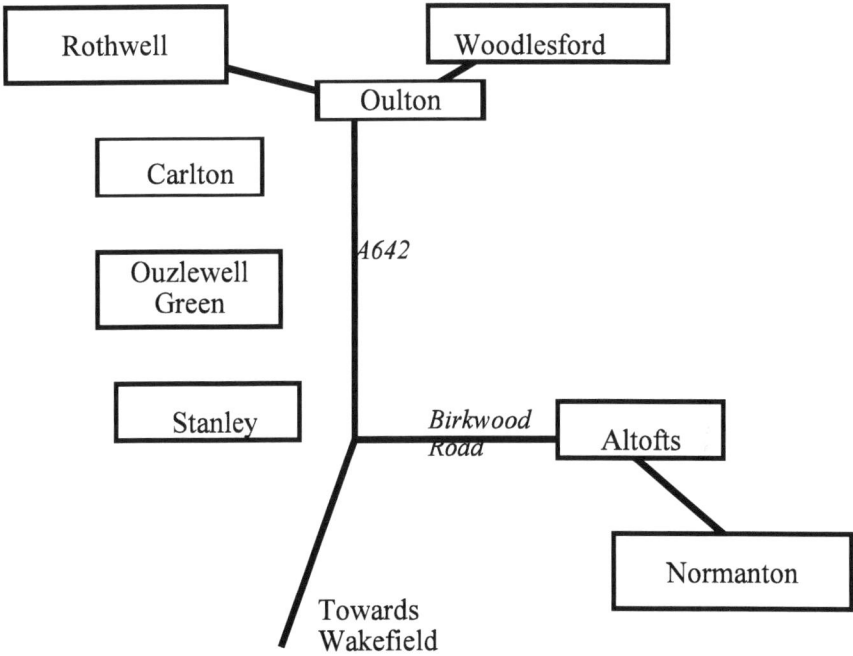

Rothwell

Woodlesford

Oulton

Carlton

Ouzlewell
Green

A642

Stanley

*Birkwood
Road*

Altofts

Normanton

Towards
Wakefield

11865052R00077

Printed in Great Britain
by Amazon